PORTRAITS
Popes, Family, and Friends

PORTRAITS
Popes, Family, and Friends

Gerald O'Collins SJ, AC

Connor Court Publishing

Published in 2019 by Connor Court Publishing

Copyright © Gerald O'Collins SJ, AC

All rights reserved. No part of this book may be reproduced or transmitted in any form or by any means, electronic or mechanical, including photocopying, recording or by any information storage and retrieval system, without prior permission in writing from the publisher.

Connor Court Publishing Pty Ltd.
PO Box 7257
Redland Bay QLD 4165
sales@connorcourt.com
www.connorcourt.com

Phone 0497900685

ISBN: 9781925826302

Cover design Maria Giordano

Printed in Australia

Dedicated to my deceased relatives and friends whose portraits remain uncreated.

Preface

Time moves faster for me nowadays and the witnesses to my life diminish. But I become even more grateful to all the living and the dead who have grounded my existence and kept me going. They went the distance, and their illuminating and encouraging presence shaped me and made me what I became.

In "The Municipal Gallery Revisited," the Irish poet W. B. Yeats recalls Lady Augusta Gregory, John Synge, and others who peopled his life: "say my glory was I had such friends." I want to say that and more about the men and women whose portraits appear in this book. These popes, relatives, and friends nourished and sustained me; my life began and ended with them.

I have already churned out three volumes of memoirs: *A Midlife Journey* (2012), *On the Left Bank of the Tiber* (2013), and *From Rome to Royal Park* (2015) (Brisbane/Leominster: Connor Court and Gracewing). Did I decode my story to produce self-serving narratives in the cause of answering two questions? How do I see myself, and how do I wish to be understood and remembered? Whatever the answers, let the focus move away to others when I reawaken memories of those who are no longer there. Recalling them and what they shared allows me to pay a debt of gratitude.

Part I will picture four popes with whom I shared Rome during my thirty-three years of teaching at the Gregorian University: St

Paul VI, John Paul I, St John Paul II, and Benedict XVI. Part II moves to four relatives: Patrick Francis and Joan O'Collins (my parents), Moira Peters (my eldest sister), and Jim O'Collins (my younger brother). Part III will include portraits of Mother (St) Teresa of Calcutta, Geoffrey Chapman, Richard Divall, Frank and Orietta Pogson Doria Pamphilj, Cardinal Avery Dulles, Jacques Dupuis, Janette ("Jan") Gray, Peter-Hans Kolvenbach, Cardinal Carlo Maria Martini, Eugene ("Gene") and Maureen McCarthy, and Peter Steele.

I would like to add other relatives and friends to this list. But twenty portraits may be enough for most readers. The subjects came from Australia, Belgium, Germany, Holland, India, Ireland, Italy, Macedonia, Poland, and the United States. Each chapter will be self-contained. Readers can start where they wish.

Faced with death, John Donne (1572–1631), one of the greatest poets who was also an outstanding preacher, said to God, "I will be made Thy music" ("Hymn to God, My God, in my Sickness"). Master of words that he was, Donne sensed the heavenly quality of music and looked forward to joining "the choir of saints." In a sermon probably preached in February 404, St Augustine of Hippo pictured our coming life similarly: "arm in arm with the angels, we shall sing the everlasting hymn, 'Alleluia.' We shall be praising God without ever growing tired." *The City of God*, Augustine's masterpiece, portrayed our future this way: God "will be the goal of our desires; he will be seen without end, loved without satiation, and praised without weariness" (22. 30). Donne and Augustine would have welcomed the much loved hymn of my fellow Jesuit, Christopher Willcock, "Let us go rejoicing to the house of the Lord."

Preface

The twenty men and women portrayed in this book went rejoicing, or at least patiently, to the house of the Lord. With choirs of angels and saints, they now sing "the everlasting hymn." Before they left us to join the heavenly company, they were for me the music of life. I spent many years in the company of some of them, much less in the case of others. Hence the chapters of this book are longer or shorter. My hope is that readers will draw inspiration and courage from all their stories.

For various kinds of help towards writing and producing this book, I wish to thank Anthony Cappello, Isaac Demase, Gesine Pogson Doria Pamphilj, Kieran Gill, Paul McMahon, Maev O'Collins, Rosemary ("Posey") O'Collins, Jin-hyuk Park, Elizabeth Parker, Bronwen Peters, James Peters, Justin Peters, Marion Peters, Mark Peters, Stewart Peters, and Alexander Ross. My warm thanks go out also to Brendan Byrne, who has made available two homilies (on Jan Gray and Peter Steele, respectively), and to John Wilkins, who has allowed me to reproduce an article on Jacques Dupuis that appeared originally in the London *Tablet* (July 11, 2015). The portrait of my sister Moira on the cover was painted by the late Paul Fitzgerald, AM. I dedicate this book to the memory of all those other relatives and friends, whose portraits I would have been delighted to include.

Jesuit Theological College, Parkville (Australia),
July 31, 2018.

Contents

Preface

Part I

1	Pope (St) Paul VI	15
2	Pope John Paul I	29
3	Pope (St) John Paul II	41
4	Pope Benedict XVI	59

Part II

5	Patrick Francis ("Frank") O'Collins	87
6	Joan O'Collins	101
7	Moira Peters	115
8	James ("Jim") Patrick O'Collins	131

Part III

9	Mother (St) Teresa of Calcutta	149
10	Geoffrey Chapman	159
11	Richard Divall	163
12	Prince Frank Pogson Doria Pamphilj	175
13	Princess Orietta Pogson Doria Pamphilj	179
14	Cardinal Avery Dulles, SJ	185
15	Jacques Dupuis, SJ	191
16	Janette ("Jan") Gray, RSM	203
17	Peter-Hans Kolvenbach, SJ	211
18	Cardinal Carlo Maria Martini, SJ	217
19	Eugene ("Gene") and Maureen McCarthy	223
20	Peter Steele, SJ	231

Index of Names　　　　　　　　　　　　247

Part I: Popes

1
St Paul VI
(Pope 1963–78)

When Paul VI was elected pope in July 1963, I was completing my final year of theological studies in a leafy suburb of Sydney and would not leave Australia for Europe until June 1964. The new pope set himself to follow the lead of John XXIII in reforming deficient traditions, bringing the Catholic Church up to date, and encouraging relations with other Christians, those of other faiths, and those of no religious beliefs at all. The Second Vatican Council had opened in October 1962, and would not finish its work before December 1965. But bishops of the world had taken charge of the Council, and the prospects for well-regulated change looked green.

During the third session of Vatican II (late 1964) and subsequent months, I was in Münster (Germany) and engaged with over twenty other Jesuits on our final, spiritual year of training. Three *periti* or theological consultors came to give us first-hand reports of Paul VI's leadership and what was happening at the Council. Otto Semmelroth discussed *Lumen Gentium* (the Constitution on the Church) and some of the drama affecting its final approval on November 21, 1964. Johannes Hirschmann spoke to us for three and a half hours about the progress being made at the Council and the prospects for the coming General Congregation of the Society of Jesus, which in July 1965 was to elect Pedro Arrupe to be the next superior general, the first Basque to serve as general since our founder, St Ignatius Loyola. Hirschmann's performance astonished me. I never imagined that someone could address me in a foreign language, continue for over three hours, and remain consistently eloquent and entertaining. Semmelroth and Hirschmann were professors of the Jesuit theological faculty of Sankt Georgen in Frankfurt.

Wilhelm Bertrams, a *peritus* at Vatican II who usually taught canon law at the Gregorian University (Rome), spent his time defending the traditional Catholic ban on artificial birth control. Along with nearly all my companions, I found his dry legalism unpersuasive. At that point, while continuing to hear them with respect, I ceased to accept the teaching of Pius XI and Pius XII against contraception. The issue was one of rational principles, not revealed truth. The arguments offered no longer seemed to support the negative conclusion.

As I learned more about Paul VI, I was delighted that he shared my affection for the Anglican Communion. Years later I made sure that photos of him with Dr Michael Ramsey, the Archbishop of Canterbury, featured among the illustrations for two books I published on Catholicism.[1] One photo showed them signing a common declaration in March 1966 which inaugurated an Anglican-Roman Catholic dialogue and also led to the opening of the Anglican Centre in Rome. That centre became part of my life during the years I taught in Rome (1973–2006). The other photo showed Paul VI

---

[1] G. O'Collins and Mario Farrugia, *Catholicism: The Story of Catholic Christianity*, 2nd edn (Oxford: Oxford University Press, 2015); G. O'Collins, *Catholicism: A Very Short Introduction*, 2nd edn (Oxford: Oxford University Press, 2017).

giving his own episcopal ring to Dr Ramsey on March 25, 1966. The Archbishop returned at once in England to give the opening address for an Easter conference in Oxford on John Henry Newman. He wore the ring just presented to him by Paul VI. Those days at Oriel College with Dr Ramsey and others linger in my memory as the most pleasant conference I have ever attended.

The director of my doctoral dissertation at the University of Cambridge (1965–68) was the (Anglican) Regius Professor of Divinity, Dennis Nineham. Dennis combined a strain of historical scepticism with High Church piety. At the end of one summer he showed me with glee a photograph of himself, his wife Ruth, and their four children talking in Rome with Paul VI, whom he called "the Holy Father."

The publication in August 1968 of the encyclical *Humanae Vitae* (Of human life) proved a watershed in thinking about Paul VI. In 1963, Pope John had set up the Pontifical Commission on Population, Family, and Birth (to be popularly called the Birth Control Commission). Three years later a clear majority on the commission expressed their conviction that it could not demonstrated that contraception is intrinsically evil. A minority, however, argued that the traditional teaching which rejected contraception should in maintained because the official Church had invested its authority in that rejection. Paul VI sided with the minority, and declared that "each and every marriage act" must be open to the transmission of life.

Years later I came to know very well one of the first members of the commission, John Marshall, by then retired as professor of neurology at the University of London. As an appendix to my *Living*

Vatican II: The 21ˢᵗ Council for the 21ˢᵗ Century[2], I added an article he wrote on the work of the commission and its aftermath. Since Catholics as whole have not been persuaded by the teaching of *Humanae Vitae,* John recognized how the encyclical has weakened and not strengthened the authority of official teaching in moral matters.

At the publication of *Humanae Vitae,* Paul VI had gone out of his way to indicate that, although teaching with authority, he made no claim to be teaching infallibly. Many national conferences of bishops, while not rejecting the papal teaching, felt free and obliged to introduce nuances that mitigated the flat rejection of contraception.

It was through teaching as a visiting professor at the Gregorian University in early 1973 that I could first see Paul VI for myself. One Sunday morning I attended Mass in St Peter's basilica, and it became a memorable, spiritual turning point. I heard a voice within me saying quietly, "Come to Rome." One can offer a natural explanation of this "voice." But from that moment any feelings of confusion about my future work faded away for good, and I decided to accept an invitation to teach fulltime at the Gregorian.

I stepped out St Peter's into the wintry sunshine to wait for the Pope to deliver his midday address from his apartment in the Apostolic Palace. Some of the crowd smiled at the man who wandered around holding up a large sign, "Don't believe the priests. Keep your money for yourselves." The shutters on a window high above St Peter's Square opened and the birdlike face of Paul VI appeared. He began by welcoming the armistice in Vietnam which had come into effect earlier that day. Then he mentioned the thirty

---

[2] Mahwah, NJ: Paulist Press, 2006.

cardinals he had just created: "They show the catholicity of the Church." I chuckled to myself: "Come, come—eight Italians out of thirty! Surely a bit unbalanced?"

I joined with the Pope in reciting the Angelus, received his blessing, and headed down the Via della Conciliazione. I crossed the Tiber, passed some Jesus people singing, laughing, and playing their guitars, threaded my way through children in the Piazza Navona, and went home in peace for lunch with the Jesuit community at the Gregorian.

When I arrived in September 1974 to begin teaching fulltime at the Gregorian, Paul VI was almost 77 years of age and had slowed down. After three years of presiding (1963–65) over the Second Vatican Council, he had worked energetically on reforming the liturgy. The new *Roman Missal* of 1970 came to be called the *Missal of Paul VI*. He pursued faithfully the task of dialogue with other Christians, Jews, followers of other faiths, and those of no religious faith. To depict that outreach, I included in *Catholicism: The Story of Catholic Christianity* a photo of Paul VI on the steps of St Peter's Basilica embracing Athenagoras, the Ecumenical Patriarch of Constantinople and head of Orthodox Christians. The Pope set himself to internationalize the Vatican offices by putting in charge of major "dicasteries" or offices such non-Italians as Cardinal Jean-Marie Villot (French) and Cardinal James Knox (Australian). He initiated a pattern of travel that John Paul II was to continue with great energy. By late 1974, Paul VI's papal pilgrimages had taken him to Colombia, India, Jerusalem, the Philippines, Sydney in Australia, Uganda, and the United Nations headquarters in New York. But he had not gone out of Italy since 1970.

He was still to publish one of his most fruitful and enduring documents: *Evangelii Nuntiandi* ("Announcing the good news") (1975). The Pope described Jesus as the first and greatest "herald" or "preacher (*praeco*)." But when the original Latin text was translated into modern languages, somehow Jesus became "the first evangelizer," and a new title was launched into popularity: Jesus the Evangelizer. Paul VI gave that document the status of an apostolic exhortation, rather than the higher grade of a papal encyclical. After the worldwide debate stirred up inside and outside the Catholic Church by his 1968 encyclical *Humanae Vitae*, he published no more encyclicals.

The Holy Year of 1975 (or year of special pilgrimage to Rome) multiplied demands on the ageing Pope. I attended the opening ceremony for the Holy Year, Midnight Mass at St Peter's 24/25 December 1974. Waiting outside in the square for an hour or so before the doors opened, the immense and impatient crowd raised a little the chilly temperature of that winter's night. An Italian nun leading a phalanx of other religious women had her shoulder down and was pushing against the legs of a tall man in front of her. He spun around and in a very British voice said: "Would you *please* stop shoving me! You won't get in any quicker, and what's more, you are making me very angry."

The film director Franco Zeffirelli, who had not yet made *Jesus of Nazareth*, directed the television coverage that night. Zeffirelli's lighting of St Peter's showed his theatrical and operatic imagination. The illumination inside the basilica raised the heat, and it was no surprise when someone near me fainted and had to be carried out. Paul VI celebrated the never-ending Mass with his usual holiness and sincerity. This was the first time I heard him preach. I was struck by the high-pitched, querulous voice with which he welcomed us in the name of Christ by repeatedly saying: "*venite* (come)."

In the course of the Holy Year, Paul VI personally ordained to the priesthood 363 deacons in the Square of St Peter's, on the Feast of Saints Peter and Paul, June 29, 1975. The ceremony began in the late afternoon and ran for hours into the evening. As the light drained out of the sky, it created special, changing effects on the red vestments that the priests, bishops, cardinals, and Pope himself wore to recall the martyrdom of two founding fathers of Christianity. All those present remembered Peter and Paul, while very many honoured in their thoughts and prayers the sheer valour of Paul VI. Crippled with arthritis, he showed the faithful courage of a living martyr as he went through the four-hour ceremony.

A year or so later I volunteered to distribute Holy Communion at a Mass that the Pope celebrated at St Paul's Outside the Walls. It may well have been on the feast of the conversion of St Paul, January 25, a day which concludes something very dear to the heart of Paul VI, the week of prayer for unity observed by many Christians around the world. When the time came for the homily, the officials put him in a chair in front of the altar, supplied a microphone, and then left him all alone—a frail figure, whose body seemed disintegrating with pain. His loneliness struck me, as he delivered his words in his normal, plaintive tone.

Paul VI spent his last summer at the papal villa in Castel Gandolfo, cared for principally by Monsignor John Magee, his Irish secretary. Magee liked to watch Westerns and ordered some videos. The Pope himself understood nothing of the traditional symbols of that genre of films: white hats and black hats, left-handers and right-handers, stereotyped ways of speaking, and the rest. But he always wanted to say something that would please and encourage others. After sitting through one Western, Paul VI turned to Magee and said: "What splendid horses! I believe you have wonderful horses in Ireland, John."

The Pope took advantage of that last stay in Castel Gandolfo to visit and pray at the nearby tomb of a cardinal, who had treated him badly many years earlier when Paul VI was a monsignor working in the Vatican. Before dying, the Pope wanted to feel more assurance that he had truly forgiven a foolish and unpleasant person.

Years later I came to know quite well a Roman-born monsignor who, from the time of John XXIII, spent years in the papal household—first working for Pope John, then right through the pontificate of Paul VI, and into the first years of John Paul II. Don Luigi had no doubts about the holiness of Pope John. But, recalling the years he spent in the Apostolic Palace, he repeatedly came back to the sanctity of Paul VI. It made me think that a pope can also be a saint in the eyes of his butler. On one occasion a small group of pilgrims were scheduled to meet the Paul VI, who at the time was suffering from flu and yet insisted on keeping the appointment. "Holiness, you could use one of your former speeches to other pilgrims," Don Luigi suggested. "No, I can't do that," the Pope replied. "I must think of something fresh and relevant to say to this new group."

I sensed that Pope John represented for Don Luigi a traditional form of holiness, while Paul VI seemed a saint for modern times. A domestic detail symbolized that difference. Pope John wore an ample night-shirt to bed, whereas Pope Paul wore pyjamas.

Despite his close friendship with Paolo (later Cardinal) Dezza, his Jesuit confessor who had been rector of the Gregorian University, Paul VI issued in 1976 a ukase against any non-Catholics teaching at the Gregorian or any other ecclesiastical university or college in Rome. This was highly embarrassing, since non-Catholic theologians had been coming as visiting professors for eight years. People in the know told me that a group of Mexican bishops were shocked that the university at which their young priests studied had the habit of inviting every year one or two teachers who were not Roman Catholics. They "got at" the old Pope to have this stopped.

On the night I heard the news, I had dinner with Dr Harry Smythe, the director of the Anglican Centre in Rome and former vicar of an Anglican church in Melbourne (Australia). Harry had just come from visiting "the Holy Father," as he always called him. It was a private visit during which Paul VI had kept a cardinal waiting. Harry brought a letter to the Pope from Dr Michael Ramsey, who recalled with gratitude their 1966 meeting. The Pope was amused at Harry's news about having just read a sign scrawled on a wall in Rome: "Viva Paolo Sesto (long live Paul VI)." The Pope laughed and remarked: "I don't think there are too many of those signs around the city. But I can't get out to see for myself."

And yet Paul VI had just issued an order forbidding the likes of Harry to teach at the Gregorian! In fact, Harry had *already* been invited to teach a course in the academic year of 1976/77. Our rector insisted that "*odiosa sunt restringenda* (odious things should be limited)," and that the ukase should apply only to future invitations. The ban, of course, led to a furor at the Secretariat for Christian Unity. Its prefect or head, Cardinal Jan Willebrands of Utrecht, quickly flew down to Rome, met with the Pope, and wrung a reluctant concession out of him to the effect that instances of non-Catholics teaching at the Gregorian should be examined individually, as had always been the case. But, in the event, it took several years before other Christian theologians (Anglican, Orthodox, or Protestant) returned as visiting professors.

Former students and professors of the Gregorian remember with gratitude, however, what Paul VI did through what was, apparently, his last official act. On the feast of the university's founder (St Ignatius Loyola), July 31, 1978, the Pope signed the document appointing Carlo Maria Martini, SJ, as the next rector of the Gregorian. Paul VI died less than a week later, on August 6, the Feast of the Transfiguration.

I was in Glasgow, leading a group of nuns on a spiritual "retreat," eight days of silence and prayer. We followed the Pope's funeral on television, a dignified ceremony on a sunny afternoon in St Peter's Square. It ended with spontaneous applause from the huge congregation when Paul VI's coffin was lifted from the ground and carried for burial into the crypt of St Peter's. Little did I imagine that I would be in St Peter's Square less than two months later, standing in the rain for the funeral Mass of Paul VI's successor.

When summing up what Paul VI did for the whole Christian Church and the world, I feel immensely grateful that he continued, completed, and implemented the work of Vatican II along the lines proposed by John XXIII. The Council yearned for leadership to come from more pastorally minded bishops, who would be with the people and for the people as genuine shepherds. Paul VI set himself to bring that about by his appointments of bishops in Spain and the United States, countries which often lacked such servant leadership. As a priest in New York said to me, "we want good shepherds, not lords of the manor."

Like his predecessors and successors, Paul VI proved the

leading apostle of peace on earth. He spoke out vigorously during his October 1965 visit to the United Nations, and pleaded with world leaders: "No more war; never again war. Peace, it is peace that must guide the destinies of people and of all mankind." He did his best to broker and bring peace in Vietnam.

Within the Catholic Church, Paul VI saw that two forms of the Roman or Latin Rite could foster disunity. Hence he ruled that the pre-Vatican II Missal (often mistakenly called the Tridentine Missal) should be replaced by the new Missal of 1970.[3] Unfortunately, however, in a personal edict of 1964 he prescribed something never mentioned by the Second Vatican Council. After the revised liturgical texts appeared (in Latin), conferences of bishops around the world were to submit their vernacular translations to be confirmed by the Holy See. This confirmation was forthcoming when the English-speaking conferences submitted their 1972 translation, But an excellent, revised translation of 1998 was peremptorily dismissed by the Vatican's Congregation for Divine Worship. New rules for translation were imposed and a different, B-class team of translators introduced. This Vatican takeover, described in a book I wrote with John Wilkins, *Lost in Translation*,[4] resulted in the stilted translation introduced in 2011, a word-for-word version in a "sacred vernacular" that falls between Latin and English.

Paul VI came from the region of Brescia, in northern Italy. His journalist father had been a member of the Italian parliament; one of his brothers became a physician and the other a lawyer. Leaders in the professional and business sectors of the city decided to keep

---

[3] It was not the Council of Trent but Pope Pius V who in 1570 published a missal, which underwent some changes right down to the pontificate of John XXIII.

[4] Collegeville, MN: Liturgical Press, 2017.

the legacy of the late Pope before the eyes of the Catholic world and encourage moves to have him officially "canonized" or declared a saint. Every year or so they organized a significant conference in Brescia on the life and work of Paul VI, and published the proceedings.

I was invited to attend one of these conferences, which was dedicated to what the late Pope had taught about the person and saving work of Jesus Christ. To my shame, I failed to speak out against Archbishop Tarcisio Bertone, still secretary of the Congregation for the Doctrine of the Faith and not yet the Cardinal Secretary of State under Benedict XVI. The CDF had shortly before published *Dominus Iesus* ("Lord Jesus"), a document from which Cardinal Martini, Cardinal Walter Kasper, and other leading figures took their distance. They were unhappy with the way this declaration characterized many Christian communities as not being "proper churches." As a theologian who taught courses every year on Jesus (who he is in himself and what he has done), I was disturbed by unfortunate ways in which *Dominus Iesus* expressed truths about Christ. At the Brescia conference, Bertone alleged: "*Dominus Iesus* represents the highpoint toward which the teaching on Paul VI was leading." The audience audibly drew its breath at this outrageous claim, but no one spoke up. I felt like saying: "Eccellenza, sono perplesso." In Italian "I am perplexed" is a polite way of saying, "I find your claim to be unacceptable and even ridiculous."

Bertone's remark made me look up again the wonderful homily about Christ that Paul VI preached in Manila on November 29, 1970: "He is the center of history and of the world. He is the one who knows us, and who loves us. He is the companion and friend of our life. He is the man of sorrows and of hope. It is he who will come and who one day will be our judge and—we hope—the everlasting fullness of our existence, our happiness." No other words sum up better the Christ-centred devotion at the heart of Paul VI's life.

2
John Paul I
(Pope 1978)

En route from Glasgow back to Rome in August 1978, I stopped in London for a couple of days and spent a memorable evening with Tom Burns, the editor of the *Tablet*, in his apartment close to Westminster Cathedral. Wearing a shirt that barely covered his stomach, Tom stood in front of his mantelpiece and put the question to a group of formally dressed guests: "Who do you think will be the next pope?" The guests included John Harriott, a brilliant writer who was still a Jesuit but would soon depart the priesthood and marry, a British diplomat who had served in Italy, and some others. Various suggestions were put forward, and nobody seemed to accept Tom's own hesitant proposal about Cardinal Albino Luciani, the Patriarch of Venice. We had our papal candidates, and gave our reasons.

The Papal Election

Home at the Gregorian a few days later, I started putting together material for Tom on the papal election. His regular Rome correspondent was away on summer holidays, and Tom asked me to fill in for a couple of weeks. Since many professors, students, and others had not yet returned to the city, I found the normal excitement of a papal conclave a little muted. However, the presence of the world's media stirred up gossip and speculation. Most of the pundits failed to list Luciani among their ten or so *papabili*, and no one suggested that he would be elected on the first full day of the conclave, Saturday August 26, 2018.

Among the people I talked with in Rome, Maurizio Flick, a tall professor from Northern Italy, was the only person to predict correctly the outcome of the papal election. Over supper in our community dining room at the Gregorian, Flick shared his prediction with me. After John Paul I was elected, I had to put the question: "Father Flick, why did you think Luciani would be chosen?" "He was the only clean (*pulito*) Italian cardinal," was the frank reply from someone who knew the Italian church very well—not least from giving a Lent retreat in the Vatican to Paul VI and many cardinals.

Among the professors of the Gregorian University itself, Luciani was quite well known. He had written a thesis for the theology faculty during the 1940s—on Blessed Antonio Rosmini Serbati (1797–1855), a philosopher, priest, and founder of the Institute of Charity, popularly known as the Rosminians. Luciani was also a relative of Felice Cappello, a saintly professor of canon law who for years was confessor to the city of Rome. When Cappello died in 1962, Luciani, by now Bishop of Vittorio Veneto, came south for the requiem Mass in the Church of St Ignatius and stayed overnight in a spare room of the Gregorian's infirmary.

The day of the election I went out for lunch with an Australian philosopher, a friend who happened to be visiting Rome with his wife and two sons. "There must have been a cosmic traffic accident," he remarked when we met at a *trattoria* hidden away in a tiny square near the Pantheon. He explained: "Just as we were about to cross the Via del Corso, a dozen or so police cars roared past and turned right towards the Tiber." I was so programmed to expect a long conclave that I failed to guess what the police already knew. A pope had been elected, and they were off to control the crowd that would quickly gather in St Peter's Square.

A waiter took our orders, and suddenly disappeared with all the other waiters. Eventually I went to see what had happened, and found them gathered around the television. "They've elected a pope," I was told. Thirty or forty minutes later when the new Pope appeared on the central balcony above the façade of St Peter's, he seemed to be quite overcome. He simply gave his blessing, smiled, waved at the crowd, and disappeared inside.

The following day, Sunday August 27, John Paul I delighted the crowd gathered in St Peter's Square for his midday blessing. Without addressing them as "my dear brothers and sisters," he simply began: "Yesterday I went off to vote without a worry in the world, and suddenly I saw the danger." His very first word, "ieri (yesterday)" drew applause from the crowd. What he then said made them all feel that they could share with him the experience— almost in the spirit of "yesterday a funny thing happened to me on my way to the forum. I was elected pope." At once I knew that Catholics and the whole world were blessed in having a pope who knew how to communicate in ordinary language and introduce vivid stories.

The Papacy

In the weeks that followed, people in Rome heard more of that lively, straightforward talk from John Paul I. He used the thirtieth anniversary of Georges Bernanos' death to recall how sixteen Carmelite nuns had been guillotined during the French Revolution.[5] As they went to the scaffold, they sang "Veni, Creator Spiritus (Come, Creator Spirit)." Naturally, as the Pope pointed out, the singing grew progressively fainter as one head after another fell under the guillotine.

Italian boys and girls were about to return to school. John Paul I used the occasion to urge them to study harder. He felt free to adapt for his purpose what the Duke of Wellington was supposed to have said long after the final defeat of Napoleon: "The battle of Waterloo was won on the playing fields of Eton." Repeating twice the two words that a largely Italian audience might have had difficulty with ("Wellington" and "Waterloo"), John Paul I told his young people that the victory at Waterloo had been prepared in the classrooms of Eton.

At another Wednesday audience, a small boy put the Pope in an embarrassing position. He made it to the dais first when John Paul I asked one of the children join him. On being asked by the Pope, "aren't you happy about going up to higher class this year?," the boy startled him by replying emphatically, "No!" When asked why, he explained: "I had a much better teacher last year." The Pope tried to save the situation for the new teacher by murmuring something to the effect that "we all have to adjust to changed situations."

For the open air Mass on Sunday September 3, when John Paul

---

[5] Bernanos immortalized the martyrdom of these French Carmelites in his 1948 *Dialogues des Carmélites*.

I officially inaugurated his pontificate, I signed on as one of the many priests who were to distribute Holy Communion to the congregation. When we filed out of St Peter's, I was delighted to find myself right behind the Pope. Across his shoulders I could take in a crowd that stretched beyond the end of St Peter's Square and down the Via della Conciliazione. One slight distraction was the Pope's haircut. Someone had trimmed his hair recently but without the usual artistry of an Italian barber. Whoever it was had left a slightly irregular line at the back of the neck. I wondered whether, before leaving Venice for the papal election, the Pope had asked his housekeeper or secretary to run the clippers over his head.

When he arrived in Rome for the conclave, Cardinal Luciani stayed with the Augustinians in the convent of St Monica, right beside St Peter's Square. The Archbishop of Sydney, Cardinal James Freeman, also spent the last few days before the conclave as a guest at St Monica's. Cardinal Luciani suggested to his Australian colleague a trip to Venice after the conclave ended and before the new pope was installed: "there will be time for us to get up there and come back."

Another thwarted plan involved an English seminarian who arrived at the Beda College (a Roman seminary for late vocations or mature aspirants to the priesthood) shortly after John Paul I died. This seminarian had been an officer in the British army. After retiring in his forties, he visited Italy. He was viewing Venice from one of the local motor boats, when he fell into conversation with a young lad. When they came ashore, the small Venetian insisted that his godfather would welcome the English stranger for afternoon tea. The visitor accepted the invitation and was astonished to discover that the godfather was the Cardinal Patriarch of Venice. Over tea and biscuits, Luciani asked the Englishman: "What do you intend to do now that you're out of the army?" "I've often thought of becoming a priest," was the answer. "Why don't you do just that?" replied the Cardinal.

The ex-army officer returned to England, and a year or so later applied to study for the priesthood. He was accepted by a bishop. While still in the UK waiting to leave for his studies at the Beda College in Rome, he learned to his delight in August 1978 that the Patriarch of Venice had been elected pope. He wrote at once to John Paul I to offer his best wishes and promise of prayers, adding: "You mightn't remember me. I'm an Englishman who came to tea with your godson one afternoon. I've finally taken your advice to become a priest and am to study at the Beda." The mature seminarian was astonished to receive a handwritten letter from the Pope a few days later: "Of course, I remember you. Please come and see me when you reach Rome."

Their meeting never took place. The Englishman was driving down to Rome and had reached Switzerland when, to his great sorrow, he heard the news about Pope Luciani's death. A year or two later he told me the whole story when I was leading a retreat or week of prayer for the students of the Beda College. The only comment that occurred to me was: "all of this means that you must become a truly great priest."

During the month of John Paul I's pontificate, a group of forty or so American bishops and one Australian archbishop were in town to attend lectures and update their theology. Although the Americans had not come to Rome for their official, five-yearly "ad limina" visit, which automatically involves a papal audience, they, nevertheless, requested a meeting with the new Pope and asked if they might bring along their lecturers as well. He agreed to see the bishops, but wanted to meet them alone, so that he could talk frankly about the challenges he had to confront. (He was to mention, specifically, the habit of taking bribes in the Vatican.) The bishops were delighted with their meeting, and I was delighted it had gone ahead. But as one of their lecturers I was sorry not to have been allowed to join them on that occasion. A few days later most of them purchased many photographs of themselves with John Paul I. At the end of their meeting with the Pope, an official photographer had entered to take the formal photos, each bishop being separately welcomed by the Pope. The visitors packed these photos into their suitcases for the people at home, some of them leaving Rome on the very night when the Pope died (September 28/29).

The Papal Death

At breakfast on September 29 I heard the bells of a nearby church tolling, but imagined that it was for an early morning funeral. Then a Jesuit brother burst into the breakfast room with the startling news that the new Pope had died.

It rained steadily on October 4, the day the funeral Mass has held in the late afternoon. In St Peter's Square I decided to stand with a group of people from the Pope's native village, Canale d'Agordo. Many of them had come south to Rome for the inaugural Mass that he celebrated just a month before under a warm sun. These men and women were desperately sad to be back so soon—on a wet afternoon for his funeral.

I could not help thinking of their married lives and the way Cardinal Luciani approached the question of birth control. In 1977, a year before he was elected pope, he published with fourteen other bishops of the Venice region a prayer book that contained some pages on the sacrament of reconciliation. The sub-section for married people encouraged them to show deep respect and mature love for each other. For those about to approach the sacrament and confess their sins, there was a question which clearly recognized the evil of abortion. As regards birth control, the question ran: "In agreement with my spouse have I given a clear and conscientious reply to the question of birth control? Have I prevented a pregnancy for selfish reasons? Have I lacked responsibility in bringing a child into the world?" And that was all. No questions were raised about methods of birth control. Over the years I regularly drew the attention of bishops and others to this sensitive and balanced teaching of Luciani and his fellow bishops.

The Aftermath

A journalist added a strange footnote to the story of Pope John Paul I. A year or so after his death, a phone-call from the porter at the Gregorian interrupted my post-lunch siesta. I came downstairs to find a vague kind of person, who intended to write a life of John Paul I and wanted to talk with me about the late Pope's connections with the Gregorian and his links with Father Felice Cappello.[6] I knew that Luciani had received a doctorate in theology from the Gregorian, and had attended the funeral of Cappello who died in 1962 and so long before I arrived from Australia. "I know very little about Pope Luciani's contacts with his relative," I told my visitor. "You should ask the secretary general of the Gregorian. He might be able to dig something out of our archives. But why write about a dead pope, whose pontificate lasted just over a month? Why not write a book on John Paul II?" I also expressed concern at the

---

[6] For an account of Felice Cappello, see my *On the Left Bank of the Tiber* (Brisbane and Leominster: Connor Court and Gracewing, 2013), 8–11.

difficulties my visitor was likely to experience when interviewing people, since he had no Italian. He brushed this aside and departed abruptly.

In 1984 this visitor, David Yallop, published his best-selling *In God's Name*, a crudely sensationalist attempt to prove that John Paul I had been murdered. That was a theory already touted by one or two trashy papers, by some right-wing extremists obsessed with masonic conspiracies, and by a couple of French writers. Several of us at the Gregorian were annoyed to be included in Yallop's acknowledgements as if we had supplied evidence in support of his theory. He had in fact not even met some of the people listed. He misspelled the name of the secretary general to whom I had referred him and with whom he had never brought up the murder theory. And he had never raised it with me either.

In 1989 John Cornwell published *A Thief in the Night* to set the record straight about the death of John Paul I,[7] who was already a sick man when elected pope. He refused to seek medical help, was neglected by others, and died of an embolism. The way some Vatican officials tampered with a couple of details concerning the Pope's death fed the fantasies of the David Yallops of this world. The reality was that Sister Vincenza, the papal housekeeper, found the Pope dead when she brought him an early morning cup of coffee. It was considered more fitting that one of his two priest secretaries should have found him. For good measure it was put about that he had died with a copy of *The Imitation of Christ* in his hands, when in fact this had been placed there after his death. Evidence controls the way Cornwell tells the whole story of papal death, but then at the end he has his own peculiar theory: John Paul I had died the

---

[7] In *Man of the Century* (New York: Henry Holt, 1997), Jonathan Kwitny concludes that Cornwell "ripped Yallop's book to shreds" (291).

previous evening. When I tackled Cornwell over this, he made a weak answer about wanting to show at least at the end of the book his own independence of judgment.

Yallop's version proposed that John Paul I had been poisoned by some villains in the Vatican—the suspects are listed—but only at the second attempt. The first attempt went astray and killed a Russian Orthodox leader, Metropolitan Nikodim of Leningrad, when he visited the Pope on September 3, 1978. Yallop reported only part of the truth. Nikodim was in poor health, and had survived several heart attacks before the one which carried him off in the presence of the John Paul I. Yallop alleged that a rumor had gone around the Vatican that Nikodim drank a cup of poisoned coffee intended for the Pope.

Unfortunately, I could never persuade my interpreter friend Miguel Arranz to write up and notarize what he told me of Nikodim's death. Miguel, a Spaniard who spoke perfect Russian, had served as an interpreter for the meeting between the Pope and Nikodim, just as he served in the same capacity for the meetings between Andrei Gromyko, the Russian Minister of Foreign Affairs, and Paul VI and later with John Paul II. "Poisoned by someone?," Miguel said to me. "That was impossible. After picking up Nikodim at the Rome airport, I was at his side all the time. Over the years he had suffered several heart attacks. Suddenly he had another attack, and collapsed right into the Pope's arms. John Paul I was horrified, and didn't know what to do. 'Give him absolution at once, Holiness,' I told him. The man's dying."

John Paul I clearly found the papacy to be a heavy burden. The Secretary of State he inherited, Cardinal Jean-Marie Villot, liked to deal with business at once. From the time Paul VI died on August

6, papers had been stuck in Villot's office. With the election of John Paul I on August 26, a flood of documents and correspondence could flow at once to the papal desk. "I need a reading machine," John Paul I commented. Publicly he presented a kindly face to the world, and became known as "the smiling Pope." I grieved that this loving shepherd and great communicator had been snatched away from us so abruptly.

One slight comfort came from the company John Paul I kept in the crypt of St Peter's Basilica. His tomb was awkward and ugly, but directly faced the graves of three admirably attractive persons, Pope John XXIII, Pope Paul VI, and Queen Christina of Sweden (who died in Rome in 1679). I found it a peaceful and happy place to pray.

3
St John Paul II
(Pope 1978–2005)

After the sudden death of John Paul I, the conclave of cardinals that met to elect his successor began on October 14, 1978. This time round, they did not seem to be in a hurry. Every now and then black smoke poured out of the chimney above the Sistine Chapel, signalling that an inconclusive ballot had taken place. The third day of the conclave coincided with the Mass in the Church of St Ignatius to open the academic year at the Gregorian University. Our rector, Father Carlo Maria Martini, announced dramatically at the end of afternoon Mass that white smoke had gone up. The new Pope had been elected at the eighth ballot.

Students rushed out of the church and reached St Peter's Square to join the excited crowd gathered under a full moon on that warm evening. Cardinal Pericle Felici, as the senior "cardinal deacon," stepped onto the central balcony and said with a rather sour expression on his face: "Annuntio vobis gaudium magnum. Habemus Papam (I announce to you a great joy. We have a Pope)." The Catholic church had a new pope and he was not an Italian, as Felici obviously expected, but Cardinal Karol Wojtyla of Cracow, Poland.

I had previously agreed to attend a reception to welcome some Anglican bishops who were visiting Rome. So it was in the Anglican Center housed in the Doria Palace that I watched on television the announcement of the new Pope and his first appearance from the balcony of St Peter's. An African bishop cried out with joy when he took "Wojtyla," as pronounced by Felici, to be an African name. "But at least he knows as a Pole what terrible suffering means," that bishop commented when I gently let him know the national origin of the successor of John Paul I.

I couldn't provide the Anglican bishops with much information about the new Pope, even though we had been together in Australia five years previously when he was flown in for the 1973 eucharistic congress in Melbourne. Cardinal Wojtyla attended some major functions of the congress, and met Mother Teresa of Calcutta for the first time. He seemed principally concerned with the Polish emigrants to Australia. After ordaining two Polish seminarians in Melbourne, he flew around the country, and even down to Hobart to meet the Poles who lived in Tasmania. Before he left Melbourne, Cardinal Wojtyla had visited a wildlife sanctuary, where, unafraid of its dangerous back legs, he fed a large kangaroo. Once I became dean of the Gregorian's theology faculty in 1985, I hung in my office a photograph of him feeding that kangaroo.

By that time I used to quote Shakespeare's words about Julius Caesar: "He doth bestride the narrow world like a colossus." John Paul II had become a universal presence, one of the best known figures and faces on the world scene.

He made over one hundred journeys outside Italy and visited at least 130 countries, in an extraordinary effort to bring the good news of Jesus Christ to the whole world. Instead of waiting for people to come to Rome, the Pope went out to them. He showed himself a tireless missionary and evangelist, trying to help Christians and others realize how Jesus is the center and source of life for every individual and the whole human race. In a special way, John Paul II reached out to young people everywhere—not least through the World Youth Days that, despite the name, ran for the better part of a week. He initiated these meetings, which drew millions of young people to Manila, Rome, Paris, and other large cities: four million to Manila, two million to Rome, and one million to Paris.

A mega pilgrim-missionary, John Paul II proved himself a super Billy Graham. But there is more to mention than world evangelism. Let me select and highlight three areas that should enter into his portrait: the Pope's outreach to other believers, his constant support of human rights and dignity, and his commitment to the diocese of Rome.

Outreach to Other Believers

For the Feast of Peter and Paul, on June 29, 2004, the Ecumenical Patriarch of Constantinople who is the spiritual head of Orthodox Christians, joined the Pope for the evening Mass in St Peter's Square. Patriarch Bartholomew preached. Right through his pontificate, John Paul II fostered relations with the Orthodox. He was sensitive to the way Greek and Russian Orthodox have believed that Catholics make the Holy Spirit subsidiary in their faith. With the hope of healing the rift, the Pope published *Dominum et Vivificantem* ("Lord and Giver of Life"). That 1986 encyclical was nothing less than a heart-felt prayer for the love, unity, and peace that only the Holy Spirit can bring. He hoped that Catholicism and Orthodoxy could come together in a new way, and re-establish the Christian heritage and character of Europe.

Back in June 1981, after Mehemet Ali Agca nearly succeeded in taking his life, John Paul II returned from hospital. He was scheduled to speak once again from the windows of his Vatican apartment to the people gathered below in St Peter's Square on June 7. That Pentecost Sunday morning I made sure of being present, along with thousands of others. I expected some dramatic words from the Pope and vigorous applause from the crowd that would encourage him along the road to full recovery. Instead of saying "grazie, grazie, grazie" to all those who had been deeply concerned to see him back, alive and well, the Pope seemed to be thinking anxiously about a delegation of Orthodox Christians visiting Rome for ceremonies in St Peter's (to commemorate the First Council of Constantinople of 381) and in St Mary Major's (to commemorate the Council of Ephesus of 431). When he asked for prayers that this ecumenical exchange would turn out happy and fruitful, he communicated anxiety about inter-church relations rather than grateful joy at being back at work.

In January 2000, at the opening of the Holy Door of St Paul's Outside the Walls, the Pope wanted the occasion to express and further the cause of Christian unity. When opening the door, he was flanked by an Orthodox leader representing the Ecumenical Patriarch and by George Carey, still Archbishop of Canterbury and head of the Anglican Communion. In his memoir *Know the Truth*, Archbishop Carey recalls how he and the Orthodox leader did something that was not on the program. The Pope asked them both to push together with him in opening the Holy Door—a wonderful symbol of a common effort towards the unity of all Christians.

Archbishop Carey was often in Rome with his wife Eileen, and they were always warmly welcomed by John Paul II. A wonderful service in 1997 commemorated St Gregory the Great sending St

Augustine to England, where he founded the See of Canterbury. For the 1997 service, Archbishop Carey once again wore the ring that Archbishop Michael Ramsey had received from Pope Paul VI and that Ramsey passed on to his successors to wear whenever they visit Rome.

From the beginning of his pontificate, John Paul II reached out not only to Orthodox and Anglicans, but also to Protestants. In 1983 he preached at the Lutheran church in Rome, on the 500th anniversary of the birth of Martin Luther. It was the first time a pope had ever preached in a Lutheran church. It was on John Paul II's watch that the Roman Catholic Church and the Lutheran World Federation jointly published a declaration on justification, or the doctrine of our being made right through the merits of Jesus Christ. This joint declaration meant very significant progress toward healing the rift between Lutherans and Roman Catholics. The head of the Council for Promoting Christian Unity, Cardinal Edward Cassidy, went up to Augsburg to represent John Paul II at the signing of the declaration on Reformation Day, 1997. Cassidy summed up the momentous nature of the event by remarking: "When I am asked on the Day of Judgment to give an account of myself, I will simply say, 'I signed the joint declaration.'"

Reaching out with head and heart to others also characterized John Paul's relations with Jews, Muslims, and others. The Simon Wiesenthal Center, a Jewish human rights center based in the United States, presented the Pope with its 2003 Humanities Award for his "lifelong friendship with the Jewish people" and for his efforts to promote Catholic-Jewish understanding. In his teaching John Paul II insisted that the special covenant made through Moses with the people of God had never been revoked. It was not rendered obsolete or inoperative by the covenant inaugurated by Christ's death and resurrection. In 1986 John Paul II visited the synagogue in Rome. He was most probably the first pope to visit a synagogue since the early days of Christianity.

He was certainly the first pope to pray in a mosque, as he did in Damascus in 2001. Years earlier, when returning from a visit to Zaire, Kenya, and some other African nations, John Paul II flew home to Rome via Morocco. At the invitation of King Hassan II, he spoke to a crowd of over 100,000 young Muslims about the religious and moral values common to Christianity and Islam. When I talked with some journalists who had flown with the Pope on the whole journey, they admitted that, "since the days when Muhammad launched Islam more than 1,300 years ago, no pope had ever been invited by a Muslim leader to do anything like that." They excused themselves for not featuring the sensational stopover in Morocco by saying, "the Pope had already left us too tired."

More than ninety times, John Paul II publicly acknowledged the grave errors and sins committed by Catholics against others. He proved an outstanding model in trying to reconcile people. Saying "sorry" does not automatically solve everything, but it is always a step in the right direction.

Perhaps the most striking inter-faith act of the Pope was his October 27, 1986 visit to Assisi with the Dalai Lama and other heads or representatives of the world's religions. It was in the town of St Francis of Assisi, the embodiment of authentic peace, that they met on the World Day of Prayer for Peace. Some Vatican officials, including certain cardinals, were outraged at the Pope's pilgrimage of prayer. Walking down a street in Rome a few days later, I picked up a flyer which showed John Paul II turning his back on Jesus and going off with Satan. I flung it into a garbage container, but now regret not have kept the flyer to remind myself and others of something which sadly recurs. It was the same with a glossy journal that advertised a film containing "very disturbing footage of John Paul II praying with heretics, schismatics, Jews, Muslims, and pagans." The advertisement accused him of "direct participation with numerous false religions," and concluded with the judgment: "All of John Paul II's actions as seen in this video have been forbidden and condemned by the Roman Catholic Church." Religious convictions can turn sour and savage in those Catholics who think that following Jesus means condemning and even hating others.

In a December 1986 address to the Roman curia, John Paul II defended his decision to pray for world peace at Assisi in company with those of other religions. He refused to abandon his conviction that "every authentic prayer is prompted by the Holy Spirit, who is mysteriously present in every human heart."

Four years later, in his encyclical letter *Redemptoris Missio* (the Mission of the Redeemer), the Pope developed this line of teaching further. He wrote: while manifested "in a special way in the Church and her members," nevertheless, the Holy Spirit's presence and activity are universal." "The Spirit's presence and activity affect not only individuals but also society and history, peoples, cultures, and religions" (no. 28). John Paul II had a vivid faith in the Holy Spirit present in every human heart and prompting authentic prayer wherever it goes up to God.

Support of Human Rights and Dignity

In his dialogue with the followers of other religions, he also broke new ground by encouraging all to work side by side for human welfare. His 1995 encyclical *Evangelium Vitae* ("the Gospel of Life") called for "the concerted efforts" of "all those who believe in the value of life." Christians and "followers of other religions" should promote together human life as "everyone's task and responsibility" (no. 91). In this encyclical, as elsewhere, John Paul II called on Christians and others to make common cause and act on their shared values in advancing human rights and dignity. This brings me to another major characteristic of his papacy: his defence of human rights and dignity.

In Rome I met many interesting, hard-working journalists, like David Smith of London's ITV. One sunny winter's day, January 2, 1982, he interviewed me on top of the Pincian Hill, the largest public garden in the city. St Peter's Basilica formed the distant backdrop. David appreciated John Paul II's appeal for civil and religious liberty in central and eastern Europe. Picking up on Joseph Stalin's question about Pius XII ("how many divisions does the Pope have?"), David insisted: "John Paul II doesn't have any army or group of parliamentary representatives to implement his policy." "Look, David," I responded, "you and I want to speak up for the truth in our world. As a journalist and a teacher, we care about justice, and hope that what we say or write will have an impact. It is certainly worthwhile for the Pope to raise his voice. Something may very well happen." And indeed it did.

One chilly morning nearly eight years later, David Smith returned with London's ITV and put me in front of a camera at the Trevi Fountain, an hour or so before Mikhail and Raissa Gorbachev were to be received by the Pope on December 1, 1989. All David wanted me to say was: "This encounter is truly an historic moment"—a normal enough platitude in a year crammed with historic moments as communist regimes collapsed one after another. I uttered my banalities and decided that this was neither the time nor the place to add, "I told you so." Garbage collectors were busily working their way around the fountain, and it was hard enough to get something audible on the tape anyway.

John Paul II consistently stood for the culture of freedom and life and against the anti-culture of oppression and death. The value he set on the sacredness of human life set him against abortion, euthanasia, and capital punishment, as well as against war as the tempting solution to international conflicts. Despite American attempts to win his support, he firmly rejected the 2003 invasion of Iraq. Addressing the diplomats accredited to the Holy See on January 12, 2004, the Pope expressed his conviction: "War never resolves conflicts between peoples." Once more he called for a global rule of law and "a more effective collective security system that gives the United Nations its proper place." The law of force should not be allowed to replace the force of law. In his teaching and personal witness, John Paul II stressed the need for forgiveness between nations and all groups at odds with each other. As he put it in his message for the World Day of Peace in 2002, "No peace without justice. No justice without forgiveness."

John Paul II's concern for the suffering peoples of the world at times expressed itself at times in his choice of cardinals, as would be the case with Pope Francis. When creating in late 2003 a batch of new cardinals, he chose three who not only belonged to cities that had never before enjoyed a cardinal as their bishop but who also represented the suffering peoples of the world. The Archbishop of Khartoum, Cardinal Gabriel Zubeir Wako, was caught up in the terrible situation that made the Sudan a scene of death, disease, and famine. By giving him a cardinal's hat, the Pope hoped to strengthen his hand in the struggle for social justice and religious freedom, as well as draw world attention to the crucifixion of the people of the Sudan.

Across in West Africa, another new cardinal, Peter Kodwo Appiah Turkson, was the bishop of Cape Coast in Ghana. Why did John Paul II pass over the capital city, Accra, and make the bishop of Cape Coast the first cardinal in the history of Ghana? To be sure, Turkson was currently the president of the bishops' conference in Ghana. But something else seems to have encouraged the Pope's choice. Cape Coast was the notorious center of the slave trade. You can still visit the fortresses that British, Dutch, and other traders built to hold African slaves before shipping them across the Atlantic. In Cape Coast Castle alone up to one thousand slaves were imprisoned, before being hurried through three outlets to the beach and the waiting ships. The Pope knew that slavery has not disappeared from our world; human trafficking continues.

The other cardinal I want to draw attention to among the group created by John Paul II in late 2003 is Cardinal Telesphore Placidus Toppo, the Archbishop of Ranchi in India. Ranchi is not one of the top cities in India, and never before had a cardinal as its archbishop. What guided the Pope's choice was the fact that Cardinal Toppo is a tribal or aboriginal Christian. There are three or four million tribal Catholics in India; socially they belong to the bottom of Indian society. By giving the red hat to the Archbishop of Ranchi, as well as to the Archbishop of Khartoum and the Bishop of Cape Coast, John Paul II showed once again his desire to promote justice for the poor and the oppressed.

Commitment to the Diocese of Rome

Then a third major theme in my portrait is the Pope's work for his own diocese. Around the city of Rome, he proved an unfailing source of encouragement to its hundreds of parishes. Whenever he was at home and not away from Rome on a pastoral journey inside or outside Italy, he tried to visit a parish every weekend and sometimes on feast days that fell during the week. He started with the poorer parishes. Before his illness (Parkinson's) put an end to all that, he had visited over three hundred parishes. He played a major role in strengthening the whole diocese and giving it what I felt it lacked when I first reached Rome in 1973: a sense of its own identity and a feeling of common responsibility towards everyone, including the sick, the homeless, the housebound, prisoners, refugees, and those suffering from drug addiction.

Let me offer one example—from the early days following John Paul's election as pope. A young priest in Rome, working to rehabilitate drug addicts, had run into sharp opposition. Church authorities intended to shut down his operation. He made a desperate eleventh-hour appeal to the new Bishop of Rome. John Paul called him in, and not only encouraged to keep working for the rehabilitation of addicts but also provided him with new facilities. The Pope added the suggestion that the priest or one of his associates might take a course in the USA to improve their techniques in the work of rehabilitation.

Beyond question, the most dramatic event during my thirty-three years in Rome came in May 1981 when the Pope was shot by Ali Agca. John Paul II underwent a well executed operation. But four days later it was still not yet clear whether he would survive. Yet he insisted on offering a Sunday message. As he could not speak to the people of Rome from the window of his apartment, he spoke by radio from a bed in the intensive care unit of the Gemelli University Hospital. "My dear brothers and sisters, I know how you are united with me these days. I am deeply grateful for your prayers, and I bless you all. I am especially close to the two persons who were wounded with me. I pray for the brother who struck me down; I forgive him sincerely. United with Christ priest and victim, I offer my sufferings for the Church and the world."

The Pope spoke slowly, somewhat breathlessly, and with pauses that more than hinted at his pain. It was the most moving broadcast I have ever listened to. I had already thought of him as a kind of spiritual John Wayne style of character, a pope of true grit, but never more so than on that Sunday in May 1981.

While he was recuperating, I sent the Pope a collection of get-well cards produced by seven-year old children at an international school in Rome. One of the John Paul's private secretaries, John Magee, wrote to me on June 12: "It was with great pleasure that I showed the letters from Sister Brigid's class to the Holy Father, and he was very much touched by the little ones' concern and very grateful for their prayers. Needless to say, we are happy to have him back at the Vatican and to see the constant improvement in his health."

Some time after John Paul II recovered, he visited Rome's high security gaol and embraced Mehemet Ali Agca, the gunman who had almost killed him. The photograph of the two of them engaged in conversation in a prison cell must rank with the most extraordinary photos of the twentieth century. I included it among the illustrations for *Catholicism: A Very Short Introduction*.

Shadows

John Paul II was heroically holy and was rightly declared a saint. But heroic holiness is not the same as perfection, which comes only in the next life. There were shadows over his papacy. From the 1980s, for instance, revelations began emerging about priests and other representatives of the Catholic Church sexually abusing minors. What came all too slowly was pastoral care and justice for the victims, as well as the removal of perpetrators from ministerial functions and their being held accountable for their crimes. The culture of clericalism and failures in canon law had allowed sexual abuse to continue and bishops to practise coverups. The tragic problem reached the very top, with John Paul II refusing to face the evidence that clearly established the sexual crimes committed over many years by Fr Marcial Maciel Degollado, the founder of the Legionaries of Christ. After being elected pope in April 2005, Benedict XVI acted quickly to bring Fr Maciel to justice and encourage long-needed reforms, including clear apologies that he made to victims of sexual abuse in Australia and the United States. Sadly an apology to the victims of predatory priests never figured among the many apologies that John Paul II made for crimes committed by members of the Catholic Church.

Sometimes John Paul II selected outstanding people for key positions. I think here of his appointing Agostino (later Cardinal) Casaroli as secretary of state and Carlo Maria (later Cardinal) Martini as Archbishop of Milan. Yet too often he could appoint most unsuitable persons, without paying attention to contrary advice and examining full dossiers on those he had in mind. He could be swayed by their devotion to the Blessed Virgin Mary, their sharing with him a passion for philosophy, their antipathy to liberation theology, or their creating institutes that bore his name. "He's a bad picker," one journalist remarked to me, and I had to agree. It surprised me that he was not more street wise about real or potential villains. After all, as a Pole he had lived through some terrible years when Nazis and Communists controlled and ravaged his country.

Many have remarked on John Paul II's failure to reform the central administration of the Catholic Church, which allowed

Vatican officials to pursue an unhealthy over-centralization. It was under his charismatic style of government that the Congregation for the Doctrine of the Faith regained its pivotal role as "the supreme congregation."

Where Paul VI wanted positions in the Roman Curia to last only five or at most ten years, under John Paul II they could last much longer: for instance, Cardinal Joseph Ratzinger as prefect of the CDF (1981–2005) and Cardinal Martinez Somalo as prefect of the Congregation for Institutes of Consecrated Life and Societies of Apostolic Life (1992–2004). Members of these congregations or consultors to them could also remain in their positions for fifteen years or more—an abuse that encouraged investing their own opinions with false authority.

Last Days

But nothing can take away the dramatic grandeur of John Paul's final days, death, and funeral. During his last two stays in the Gemelli Hospital in early 2005, a hillside right outside was covered with the stands of TV and radio networks. They looked right across at the fifth floor of the hospital where the Pope was confined to bed. The world's media wanted to be there and cover the last weeks in the life of John Paul II, someone they had come to know and cherish deeply. He was an international celebrity, among the best known faces around the globe.

About half an hour before he went home from his first stay in the clinic, I was being interviewed by a tall Australian blond, who ended by asking how he would go back to the Vatican. "Diana," I assured her, "he's not going home in his pajamas and dressing gown. He'll be heading home dressed like the Pope and sitting up." He did just that and was driven back to the Vatican in his popemobile, a special vehicle with large windows. John Paul II waved to people along the road, and the applause from the Romans showed how much they cared for him and were emotionally involved in his last sickness.

After a second stay in the Gemelli, the Pope went home to the Vatican for the Holy Week and Easter Sunday of 2005. But he was unable to attend the ceremonies, let alone preside at them. He could not speak when he was moved to the window of his apartment to give the Easter Sunday blessing to the vast crowd gathered in St Peter's Square. Parkinson's disease had finally reduced him to silence. Sir John Gielgud, an outstanding actor on the stage or in films, remarked about John Paul II: "I have never heard anyone deliver his lines with better timing." That wonderful voice had fallen silent forever, and I thought: "That's it. He will be ready now to go home to God."

The following Saturday, April 2, at 9.37 p.m., John Paul II died at home in the Vatican. Below his apartment thousands of young people had been keeping vigil: holding candles, singing hymns, and praying in various languages. Some were weeping, others rejoicing that the 84-year-old Pope had been delivered from so much pain and could leave his suffering behind and enjoy eternal happiness with God.

From the TV platform of the BBC, high up on the Janiculum hill which overlooks St Peter's Square, I followed this very public death, and heard the ten-ton bell of St Peter's tolling the passing of the Pope. They were amazing days to be in Rome. A flood of people poured into the city. Above all, there were thousands of young people who spontaneously converged on the city. They wanted to pay their last respects to an old friend whom they cherished. Reportedly the

PORTRAITS, Popes, Family, and Friends

last whispered message from John Paul II before he fell unconscious was for the young: "I went looking for you. You came to me, and for that I thank you."

The Pope died on a Saturday evening. On the Monday afternoon, he was carried out of the Vatican Palace and through St Peter's Square, held up high in an open casket. He seemed like a Viking king passing through the midst of his people to the last rites. They placed his body in front of the main altar of St Peter's Basilica—to lie there in state for the world to visit.

From the Monday evening through to Thursday, a gigantic column of people queued up for ten or twelve hours or even longer, before they could enter St Peter's and file past the catafalque to pray and pay their final respects. The column, which moved along between wooden barriers, was at least twenty-five people across and ran back for more than mile. Up to two million people came to visit John Paul II lying in state.

On Friday, April 9, the world stood still for the last rites of the Pope, held against the façade of St Peter's Basilica. There has never been a papal funeral like that one. On TV two billion people followed the funeral Mass, guided brilliantly by the master of ceremonies (Archbishop Piero Marini) and presided over with dignity and devotion by Cardinal Joseph Ratzinger, the dean of the College of Cardinals. In Rome itself half a million packed into St Peter's Square and the adjacent streets. In other squares around the city, huge screens let two million more people follow the ceremony.

There were numerous touching moments in the funeral Mass and the concluding rites. When the time for Holy Communion came, the first in line to receive Communion from Cardinal Ratzinger was a white-haired, 90-year-old man in a wheel chair, Brother Roger

Schutz of Taizé, an ecumenical center in northern France that has been become a powerful place of pilgrimage for young people. As a young bishop during the Second Vatican Council (1962–65), John Paul II came to know Brother Roger and other monks of Taizé through praying and eating with them in their small apartment in Doria Palace, Rome. During summer, the fields surrounding the monastery fill up with tents, and young men and women learn to love the meditative music of the eighty or so monks. At evening prayer in August 2005, a little over four months after the funeral of John Paul II, a deranged person stabbed Brother Roger to death.

For many of us the most moving moment during the papal funeral came right at the end when members of the Swiss Guard lifted the simple, wooden coffin up from the ground in front of the altar. They carried John Paul II slowly and solemnly past the rows of presidents, monarchs, princes, prime ministers, and other powerful political leaders of our world. It was as if the dead Pope was preaching his last sermon to all those celebrities who live lives of pomp and circumstance: "You too are mortal. You too must face death and go home to God." When those bearing the coffin reached the top of the steps and were about to disappear through the huge, bronze doors into St Peter's Basilica, they paused and turned the coffin around to face the audience. It seemed as though they were giving John Paul II one last look at Rome and the world that he loved so much. Then they took him inside and buried him in the crypt of St Peter's, right next to his immediate predecessors, Pope Paul VI and Pope John Paul I, and close to the tomb of Queen Christina of Sweden.

The funeral was over, and the political and religious leaders of the world began moving away from the steps of St Peter's. At the end only one solitary figure remained standing there, alone in the section for special guests: Rabbi Elio Toaff of Rome. The old man, a

Holocaust survivor, stood in his black jacket and hat, praying for his friend, Pope John Paul II. Then a young cleric slipped along the row of seats to take the rabbi's arm and accompany him into St Peter's and out the back to his car.

Like Rabbi Toaff, John Paul II had set himself to remind the human race of the heart of the matter. Our happiness and even survival depend on faith in God and the core values expressed by the Ten Commandments.

4

Benedict XVI (Pope 2005–2013)

The conclave to elect a successor to St John Paul II began on Monday April 18, 2005, and 115 cardinals were locked up—that is what "conclave" means—for the election. I was on camera with the BBC when they filed into the Sistine Chapel and took an oath to preserve secrecy about the proceedings. I could not help remarking to Brian Hanrahan, the BBC presenter: "Brian, there are 115 cardinals going in to vote, and 44 of them either studied at the Gregorian University or taught there. It's about time the papacy came back to the Gregorian."

In the event, the papacy did "come back" to "the Greg", since as a visiting professor from the University of Regensburg, Joseph Ratzinger had taught an optional course on the Eucharist at the Gregorian in the fall of 1972. In 1977, Paul VI named him archbishop of Munich and three months later a cardinal. When John Paul II called Ratzinger to Rome in November 1981 to become prefect of the Congregation for the Doctrine of the Faith (CDF), I suggested to the dean of theology at the Gregorian, René Latourelle: "Why don't we invite Cardinal Ratzinger to teach an optional course each year? I'm sure he would like to keep his hand in as a theology professor."

Latourelle nodded agreement, paused, and then said: "A good idea. But it would make other cardinals jealous." Ratzinger might have become a regular visiting professor at the Gregorian from 1982. His brief stint there in late 1972 did, however, qualify him to have been a teacher at the "Greg."

Getting to Know Ratzinger

When following the work of the Second Vatican Council from a distance, first in Australia (1962–63) and then in Germany and England (1964–65), I appreciated the valuable insights the young Ratzinger contributed as a *peritus* (an official expert) and consultor to Cardinal Josef Frings of Cologne. Ratzinger's breadth of vision on revelation, tradition, and theology was displayed in what he wrote for the five-volume *Commentary on the Documents of Vatican II* edited by Herbert Vorgrimler.[8] Years later a colleague of mine at the Gregorian University, Jared Wicks, would translate into English for the *Gregorianum* (2008) and evaluate very positively six texts, produced by the young Ratzinger for Cardinal Frings and others, which fed into the Vatican II debates and the final crafting of some documents. In *My Journal of the Council*, Yves Congar, the outstanding theological expert at the Council, mentions Ratzinger's input and not least his contribution to the drafting and revising of the final text of the Decree on the Church's Missionary Activity (*Ad Gentes*).

In June 1968 I came back for a third summer semester at the University of Tübingen and found lodgings right next door to Ratzinger's house on the Friedrich-Dannenmann-Strasse. The previous year he had delivered for "hearers of all faculties" a

---

[8] London: Burns & Oates, 1967–69.

marvellous series of lectures on the Apostles' Creed, *Introduction to Christianity*, which quickly appeared in German, English, and other languages. One Sunday I went with him and his sister Maria (who acted as his housekeeper) to hear a perfect performance of Mozart's Mass in C minor at a baroque church in Zwiefalten, a delightful village near Tübingen. I tried to make conversation with Maria: "That was an excellent book on revelation and tradition which your brother wrote with Karl Rahner." "Never heard of it," she admitted cheerfully. But she did know, and was a big fan of, his best-selling book on the Creed. The royalties were rolling in. Herr Professor and Maria were hoping to get a house in Bavaria on the proceeds, as they later did.

Soon after I arrived in the summer of 1968, I met Ratzinger on the street. As had happened the year before, he was friendly—he asked about my work. I asked about his. After that we continued to chat and I got the impression that he was a shy character. There was always an air of formality about the way he looked. You would not see him in jeans and a T-shirt. He normally wore a dark suit and a dark tie. Unlike some of the local professors, he never seemed too big for his boots. He did not have a great sense of humour, but he was witty. If I got something wrong in my imperfect German, he might tease me for it.

Ratzinger's work seemed very important to him; even his social circle consisted mainly of PhD students. His favourite restaurant was "the Museum" on the Wilhelm-Strasse, where you could eat well on Wiener schnitzel and dumplings, washed down with Bavarian beer and local wine. Ratzinger had long lunches there with his students, deliberating over matters of theological research.

We had different theological interests; so I went to only one or two of his lectures. But they were a revelation in terms of his character. When I met him on the street, he was consistently quiet, but on the podium he was transformed: sure of his ground, able to beef up his arguments and deliver his words with authority. At the University of Cambridge, where I wrote my own PhD (1965–68), some theologians could sit on the fence intellectually. But at the University of Tübingen I met in Ratzinger someone not at all afraid to nail his colours to the mast.

I never imagined that Ratzinger would one day become pope, but I did think he would make it to be a bishop. There was a tradition in Germany of appointing academics who had done very well, very fast.

After the summer of 1968, our paths crossed only once before he arrived in Rome to head the CDF. Latourelle and I co-edited a volume in collaboration, *Problems and Perspectives of Fundamental Theology*.[9] Our stellar group of contributors included Juan Alfaro, Avery Dulles, Carlo Maria Martini, Karl Rahner, and Jean-Pierre Torrell. I had hoped to include a chapter by Johann Baptist Metz. He had just published (in its original German) *Faith in History and Society: Toward a Practical Fundamental Theology*, a book inspired by what he called "political theology," a more sophisticated, European counterpart to Latin American liberation theology. But his appointment to a chair at the University of Munich was vetoed by Ratzinger, then Archbishop of Munich. The veto upset Metz and distracted him from writing the chapter he had initially agreed to supply.

Once Ratzinger moved to the eternal city, our paths crossed regularly. When John Paul II visited the United Kingdom in 1982,

---

[9] New York: Paulist Press, 1982; Italian original 1980.

the Archbishop of Canterbury, Robert Runcie, welcomed him at Canterbury Cathedral and later flew down to Rome to return the visit. On that occasion, Ratzinger and I were both guests at a small dinner party in the Anglican center. During the meal I could not help noticing the frosty relationship between Orietta Doria Pamphilj and Ratzinger. Her open-minded attitude did not sit well with him. There seemed little love lost between the tall Italian princess and the chunky German cardinal.

Ratzinger came to the Gregorian for a public lecture by a New Testament scholar and retired Lutheran bishop, Eduard Lohse. Before a huge audience Lohse discussed what the apostle Paul contributed to esteem for the ministry of Peter that emerged in the first century. He got close to arguing that Paul was the principal architect of the Petrine office. Ratzinger sat in the front row and occasionally nodded off. In 1980 he and Lohse had joined forces in welcoming John Paul II when he visited to Germany—Ratzinger as cardinal archbishop of Munich and Lohse as the presiding Lutheran bishop in West Germany.

The cardinal gave a keynote address at a symposium on the Scriptures held at the Gregorian in April 1992. The first part of his lecture traced with accurate fairness the history of Catholic biblical scholarship up to the Second Vatican Council, which closed in December 1965. Then he continued with the inflammatory statement: "After the Council, Catholic exegesis capitulated to the world." I was sitting with a Spanish scriptural scholar. We both began writing down the names of leading Catholic commentators on the Bible who had allegedly "capitulated to the world": Raymond Brown, Joseph Fitzmyer, Joachim Gnilka, Xavier Léon-Dufour, Carlo Maria Martini, Roland Murphy, Rudolf Schnackenburg, Heinz Schürmann, Albert Vanhoye, and other distinguished scholars. After the symposium ended, I tackled the Cardinal's secretary: "What on earth was all that about?" "He was only trying to be provocative," was the loyal if lame response. Back in his days at the University of Tübingen (1966–69) Professor Ratzinger left me uneasy with his seeming disdain for biblical scholarship. That attitude had not changed.

An ironical aftermath came with the superb and very well received 1993 document by the Pontifical Biblical Commission (PBC), *The Interpretation of the Bible in the Church*. As prefect of the CDF, Cardinal Ratzinger was automatically president of the PBC and wrote the preface for their latest text. The slim volume also contained a beautiful and very positive address given by John Paul II on the occasion of the document being presented. The address had been prepared for the Pope by the secretary of the PBC, Father (later Cardinal) Albert Vanhoye, one of those postconciliar exegetes who had "capitulated to the world."

In a two-volume work that he began writing in 2003 and so two years before he was elected to the papacy, *Jesus of Nazareth* (2007, 2011), Ratzinger continued to show his discomfort with biblical scholarship and claimed that such "critical scholarship has nothing further to offer." Volume one of *Jesus of Nazareth*, even more than volume two, became a best seller everywhere. When I passed through airports on international flights, it regularly showed up at the bookstores. It sold more than two million copies in various languages. I evaluate this volume in an appendix to this chapter.

Many Latin American students—and others—had been upset by the 1984 "Instruction on Certain Aspects of the Theology of Liberation," issued by the CDF and condemning liberation theology. The document often seemed to caricature a theology which was deeply committed to justice for the oppressed. Cardinal Ratzinger put his case against any and all attempts to distinguish Marxist analysis from Marxist ideology. When he accused the liberation theologians of preferring justice to faith, he appeared to support faith without justice.

None of us were aware that Pope John Paul II had become dissatisfied with the negative tone of the 1984 instruction. He asked Cardinal Roger Etchegaray, the head of the Pontifical Commission for Justice and Peace, to draft a second text to counterbalance the first. Two years later the CDF published a friendly, positive document, "Instruction on Christian Liberty and Liberation." A journalist with good connections assured me that the initiative for the 1986 instruction came from Etchegaray himself, supported by three Brazilian cardinals. They persuaded the Pope to request and accept the second, more favourable, document. In September 1993, John Paul II, when visiting Riga (Latvia), used some Marxist terminology and spoke of "Marxism's kernel of truth," in that it analysed with partial correctness the social and economic situation, even while proposing unacceptable solutions.

Beyond question, it was through the trial in which the CDF involved a Belgian theologian, Jacques Dupuis (1923–2004), that I came to know Cardinal Ratzinger most dramatically. As the official consultor to Dupuis and his advocate when he finally met the Cardinal, I experienced the case from the inside, and would eventually take a chapter (the longest in the book) to tell the whole story in *On the Left Bank of the Tiber*.[10] Here I want to recall only being painfully astonished by something Ratzinger published and then by something he said.

---

[10] Brisbane/Leominster: Connor Court/Gracewing, 2013.

When news of the proceedings against Dupuis (over his book *Toward a Christian Theology of Religious Pluralism*) broke, Cardinal Franz König, the retired Archbishop of Vienna and a long time supporter of interfaith dialogue, published on January 16, 1999 in the London *Tablet* a two-page article entitled "In Defence of Fr Dupuis." König called the book "masterly," and stated that he had been "fascinated" by it. He followed up the article by a long interview in the February number of an Italian monthly edited by a former Italian prime minister (Giulio Andreotti), *Trenta Giorni*. König's powerful advocacy could not be ignored.

Shortly after the interview appeared, the *Tablet* (March 13, 1999) carried an English translation of an open letter addressed to Cardinal König and signed by Cardinal Ratzinger, who had invited the London weekly to publish it. Ratzinger began by expressing his "astonishment" and "sadness" over the article König had published. He went on to claim that the CDF's action "had consisted *simply* in sending some confidential questions to Fr Dupuis *and nothing more than that*" (emphasis added). He rejected König's statement that the CDF "may well suspect him [Dupuis] of directly or indirectly violating Church teaching."

I read Ratzinger's assertions with my own astonishment and sadness. What Dupuis had received the previous October in a nine page, single-spaced document from the CDF included much more than "some confidential questions." The document did contain some questions. But it began with fierce charges about the orthodoxy of Dupuis's book; he was explicitly accused of directly violating Church teaching. It made me sad that Cardinal Ratzinger (or someone at the CDF writing in his name) could be so economical with the truth in a public letter to a very prominent cardinal, who had been a leading figure at the Second Vatican

Council and who came very close to being elected pope in October 1978.

Ratzinger's use of the word "dialogue" also astonished me. The letter to König repeatedly referred to the CDF's desire to "dialogue" with Dupuis and to "consult him personally." "If this is dialogue," I thought, "I would hate to see confrontation." Cardinal Ratzinger had never contacted Dupuis directly by phone or letter, let alone asked him to sit down for a discussion. The set of theses against Dupuis's book were delivered to him indirectly—by the superior general of the Jesuits, Fr Peter-Hans Kolvenbach. When Dupuis submitted two lengthy responses, he received no acknowledgment from the CDF. It was only on September 4, 2000 that Dupuis finally met Ratzinger face to face at the CDF building, which faces what is still called "the Piazza of the Holy Office."

As the one consultor whom Dupuis was allowed, I attended that meeting and joined forces with Kolvenbach in successfully challenging the "notification" the CDF had already prepared against Dupuis's book. Before adjourning the meeting, Ratzinger asked Dupuis whether he would help the CDF improve the text to produce a new "notification." "But I have already sent you 260 pages," Dupuis protested. He looked astonished when Ratzinger retorted: "You can't expect us to read and study all that material." It has never ceased to grieve and anger me that a cardinal, who in his role of prefect acted as the supreme accuser and supreme judge in the CDF, could so readily excuse himself from examining what a defendant had written in reply to the accusations and questions sent him by the CDF. I could only imagine the uproar if a senior judge were to make a similar admission at a court session in the USA, England, or Australia—not to mention other countries.

The Pontificate of Benedict XVI

After John Paul II died in 2005, two American Jesuit friends, Daniel Kendall and Jeffrey LaBelle, worked with me in sifting through the late pope's official teaching. It included well over seventy thousand pages of encyclicals (fourteen of them published from 1979 to 2003), apostolic exhortations and letters, homilies, addresses, and other published texts. Paulist Press generously provided the substantial payment that the Vatican Press had surprisingly, even scandalously, begun demanding for reproducing papal teaching. In 2007, we published *John Paul II: A Reader*, a work divided into twelve chapters—beginning with his teaching on the divine self-revelation in the person and work of Jesus Christ and ending with his teaching on Christian spirituality.[11]

The legacy of teaching that Benedict XVI left as pope 2005–2013 (and not as theologian down to 2005) is much leaner. Unlike John Paul II who was elected to the See of Peter at the age of 58, Benedict came to the papacy aged 78. John Paul II's papacy lasted for over 26 years, whereas Benedict resigned before completing eight years on the papal throne. In a program for Polish national television that was aired on October 16, 2005, the anniversary of the election of John Paul II in1978, Benedict made it clear that he did not intend to compete with his predecessor. He remarked: "I consider it my essential and personal mission not so much to produce many new documents but to see to it that [John Paul II's] documents are assimilated, because they are a very rich treasure, the authentic interpretation of Vatican II."

Pope Benedict published four encyclical letters: *Deus Caritas Est* ("God is Love") of December 25, 2005, *Spe Salvi* ("Saved

---

[11] Mahwah, NJ: Paulist Press, 2007.

by Hope") of November 30, 2007, *Caritas in Veritate* ("Love in Truth") of June 29, 2009, and *Lumen Fidei* ("the Light of Faith"), substantially written by Benedict but published by Pope Francis on June 29, 2013. I should also mention two significant exhortations, the first published in 2007 and the second in 2010: *Sacramentum Caritatis* ("the Sacrament of Love") on the Eucharist, and *Verbum Domini* ("the Word of the Lord") on the Scriptures as used in liturgical practice and preaching.

Caritas in Veritate took up issues like globalisation, hunger and poverty, climate change, and social equity between nations. These issues were to shape the teaching of Pope Francis, not least his 2016 encyclical on ecology and climate, *Laudato Si'* ("Praised be [to you, my Lord"]). Benedict's concern to "go green before it is too late" showed through his address to 300,000 young people gathered in Loreto at the end of August 2007. Convinced that "being green is being pro-life," he installed solar panels on the Vatican roof.

The finest expression of Benedict's social teaching came in an address to the General Assembly of the United Nations in April 2008. He emphasized seven themes, beginning with the obligation of the international community not to close its eyes to "grave and sustained violations of human rights." He ended by insisting on dialogue between religions as serving the common good.

BBC television invited me to comment on the Pope's address to the UN. I expressed satisfaction over his general principles that could easily be supported by hard data and translated into specific examples. I pointed out, for example, how his appeal for international action to reduce world hunger could be backed up: nearly a billion people remained chronically hungry, as well as lacking safe water to drink. As regards his call for peace, I argued that a more secure world would come only through promoting human rights and eliminating gross inequalities. If you want peace, work for justice. Those who remain oppressed, economically and politically, will turn to violence.

The BBC also brought me to their studios in White City (London) when Pope Benedict made his first pilgrimage to Africa by visiting Angola and the Cameroon in March 2009. He called for an end to years of horribly destructive wars and civil strife. With many African countries ravaged by AIDS, journalists who travelled with Benedict raised the question of using condoms to prevent spreading the pandemic. Unlike several cardinals, the Pope would never accept such use, even as "the lesser of two evils." In my BBC interview I recalled the progress made in Uganda, where the Christian churches encouraged the radical changes in social attitudes and practice needed to check the spread of AIDS. With the slogan "zero grazing," they called on men to be faithful to their wives. Only the naïve thought that, by simply distributing condoms everywhere, the tragedy of AIDS could be overcome. Nevertheless, I could not condemn husbands using condoms when they were already infected and did not want to infect their wives. "'Thou shalt not kill' trumps everything," I proposed. For a week the BBC quoted that statement.

In May 2007, Pope Benedict addressed a letter to the Catholics in China and published it in several languages, including traditional and modern Chinese. It revealed a deep desire to normalize relations with the government of China and to secure unity between Catholics who were officially registered with the state and those who belonged to clandestine communities. The letter showed an openness and flexibility that had not always characterized the Vatican stance towards Communist China in the post-World War II period.

Part I: Popes

In opening Benedict's trilogy on love, hope, and faith, *Deus Caritas Est* took papal teaching forward by dealing with *erōs* (the love of desire) and *agapē* (self-giving love) and arguing that they differ from and also match each other. When presenting his arresting reflections on how (a) love as need or love as receiving complements (b) love as benevolence or love as giving, the Pope quoted a surprising team of authors—not only the Song of Songs, St Augustine of Hippo, and St Gregory the Great, but also Aristotle, Descartes, Nietzsche, and Virgil. When he turned to expound the story of Adam and Eve and the erotic attraction between the sexes, Benedict cited something I had studied many years before. In the *Symposium*, Plato proposed a myth which pictured the human being as originally spherical—that is to say, complete, self-sufficient, not divided as male and female, and so without a sexual partner. Now, when "split in two by Zeus, he longs for his other half, striving with all his being to possess it and thus regain his integrity" (*Deus Caritas Est*, 11).

Spe Salvi, the first papal encyclical ever written on hope, is peppered with references and insights of every kind: biblical, doctrinal, spiritual, philosophical, historical, and artistic. It appeals to some great voices of the Christian tradition: from St Augustine to Cardinal Nguyen Van Thuan, a prisoner for thirteen years in Vietnam, nine of them spent in solitary confinement. Like a book on hope, *Eschatology: Death and Eternal Life* (which Ratzinger originally published in 1977), *Spe Salvi* draws on a Jewish thinker from the twentieth-century Frankfurt School, Theodor Adorno, to picture a justice that will come through the resurrection of the dead. But, unlike that book, it neither develops a theology of death nor attends to the immortality of the soul.

For all its richness, Pope Benedict's second encyclical does not include everything one might expect. It passes over in silence the Second Vatican Council which concluded by issuing its longest document *Gaudium et Spes* ("*Joy and Hope*") and declaring: "the future of humanity lies in the hands of those who are strong enough to provide coming generations with reasons for living *and hoping*" (no. 31). Nor does the encyclical mention the Holy Spirit, whose powerful presence works to bring all things to final salvation (Romans 8:23). These are surprising omissions. I wrote a full review of *Spe Salvi* for *America* magazine (January 21–28, 2008).

Lumen Fidei completes the trilogy on love, hope, and faith—a trilogy that no pope had ever before attempted. But this final encyclical does not shine with the brilliant observations that characterized Ratzinger's early exploration of faith delivered at the University of Tübingen, *Introduction to Christianity*.

On October 7. 2012, less than six months before he resigned the papacy, Benedict added two further names to the list of doctors of the Church: St John of Avila and St Hildegard of Bingen. This continued the initiative of Paul VI, who put two women on this official list: St Catherine of Siena and St Teresa of Avila. John Paul II added the name of St Thérèse of Lisieux. Of the 36 doctors of the Church, four are now women. When Thérèse of Lisieux was put on this prestigious list, a journalist phoned me at the Gregorian University and said: "Some of your colleagues don't like this papal nomination. Thérèse led a short, quiet life in a Carmelite monastery out in the French countryside. What's she doing alongside Augustine, Thomas Aquinas, and Teresa of Avila?" "Becoming a doctor of the Church," I assured the journalist, "is not the posthumous award of a PhD. After her death, Thérèse's writings have been read by millions of Christians. She continues to have a worldwide influence. That's what really matters."

Part I: Popes

Unfortunate Sayings and Doings

Any honest sketch of Benedict XVI's pontificate must include some things that he said and did that were doubtful, disappointing, or worse. Let me recall five such examples.

(1)   In an address delivered at the University of Regensburg (September 12, 2006), he quoted some unfortunate remarks about Muhammad, which provoked angry reactions from Muslims. He had cited a 14th century, Byzantine emperor as saying that Muhammad brought "only evil and inhuman things" into the world. Subsequently the Pope said that these words from Manuel II Palaeologus did not reflect his own personal views. He wanted only to encourage interreligious dialogue "with great respect."

If Archbishop Michael Fitzgerald had seen the speech beforehand, he would have strongly urged Pope Benedict to omit the offensive section. But earlier that year Fitzgerald had been unfairly exiled to Cairo as papal nuncio to Egypt (2006–2012). Secretary (1987–2002) and then president (2002–2006) of the Pontifical Council for Interreligious Dialogue, he was one of the foremost Catholic experts on relations with Islam. What Benedict over and over again desperately needed were close advisers like Fitzgerald, who would say "no" to him and eliminate in advance remarks that were insensitive or plainly mistaken. Benedict's secretary of state, Cardinal Tarcisio Bertone, was a prelate of limited capacity and experience, and had a less than distinguished career as secretary of the CDF. Reportedly a group of German cardinals visited Benedict in the papal summer residence in Castel Gandolfo and begged him to find another secretary of state. But the Pope insisted on keeping Bertone at his side. "Der Mensch bleibt (the man stays [with me])," he retorted.

Sometime late in 2006, I pointed out to a journalist who had been present at Pope Benedict's address that Regensburg was an unfortunate place to quote anti-Muhammad sentiments. Right in the middle of the city a bulky statue commemorates Don John of Austria, who was born there and eventually led the Christian forces to victory over the Muslims at the Battle of Lepanto in 1571. "None of us ever noticed that statue," the journalist commented ruefully. "Otherwise," he added, "it would have featured in what we wrote."

(2) Second, within Christian circles, Benedict displeased Anglican leaders by introducing on November 4, 2009 a special "ordinariate," which enables Anglicans to enter into communion with the Catholic Church but retain Anglican features. In particular, they can maintain some parish structures and enjoy their own bishop. This move aimed at allowing Anglicans to preserve their particular "heritage." It was hard to identify what that might mean concretely. All honour to the Book of Common Prayer, treasured by Anglicans but now replaced normally by modern texts. Some gems of the Anglican heritage have long ago entered the practice of many Christian churches: for instance, the Advent service of nine lessons and carols. Married clergy have been another significant feature of the Anglican heritage. Numerous Anglican priests, who have entered full communion with Rome, have become Catholic clergy and function wonderfully well in regular parishes. Another precious feature of the Anglican heritage has been a liturgical dignity that includes an excellent proclamation of the Scriptures. When former Anglican clergy enter the ordinary structures of Catholic parish life, they spread that excellence everywhere. The united but separate structure of the Anglican ordinariate seems at best unnecessary and at worst divisive.

(3) Third, Pope Benedict gave a high priority to bringing back into Catholic unity a tiny, schismatic group, the Priestly Fraternity or Society of St Pius X. It had been created by Archbishop Marcel Lefebvre in 1970 as a counter to the Second Vatican Council and its implementation. Lefebvre questioned or simply rejected key teachings of Vatican II: freedom of conscience, ecumenical and interreligious dialogue, the common priesthood of all the baptized, the collegiality or co-responsibility of bishops "with Peter and under Peter," and liturgical reform.

Then in 1988 Lefebvre illicitly consecrated four bishops, defiantly acting against what he considered liberal, "neo-Protestant" tendencies even among members of the Catholic hierarchy. The provisions of canon law meant that Lefebvre and the four bishops incurred automatic excommunication. In January 2009 and so after the death of Lefebvre (1991), in the hope that all members of the Society of St Pius X would return to full communion with the Catholic Church, Pope Benedict lifted the excommunication, but with little effect on the members of the Society. Under its superior general (one of the four bishops ordained by Lefebvre), the Swiss-born Bishop Bernard Follay, it has continued to reject key teaching of Vatican II, even if a few members have trickled back into Catholic communion.

The lifting of the excommunication caused international uproar, above all because another of the four bishops, Richard Williamson, took his revisionist view of history as far as Holocaust denial. His first publicly known denial that Jews died in Nazi gas chambers hit the headlines in 1989 during a trip to Canada, and he repeated his denials on Swedish television in November 2008. In 2010 a German court was to fine him 10,000 euros for unrelentingly and very publicly challenging the historical reality of the murder of nearly six million Jews.[12] In a March 2009 letter addressed to the bishops of the world, Pope Benedict tried in vain to justify his lifting of the excommunication.

A 2010 volume, published as no. 236 in the famous *Quaestiones Disputatae* ("Disputed Questions") series and edited by Professor Peter Hünermann of the University of Tübingen, discussed issues of church governance and teaching raised by the Williamson affair. While respecting the pastoral responsibility of the Pope to bring back splinter groups, the contributors also raised critical questions about the direction of the Church under Benedict's leadership. They highlighted the roots of Lefebvre's movement in the antidemocratic, anti-Semitic milieu of a late nineteenth- and early twentieth-century movement, *Action Francaise*.

Traditionalist ideology shaped the outlook of Lefebvre and his associates. They repudiated the Church's "dialogue with the world," initiated by Pope John XXIII and Vatican II and spectacularly endorsed by John Paul II right from his first encyclical, *Redemptor Hominis* ("the Redeemer of the Human Person") of 1979. The volume edited by Hünermann made it clear that the whole controversy concerned nothing less than a comprehensive struggle over Vatican II and its lasting meaning for the Church and the world.

Hünermann himself made a convincing case that there were no legitimate grounds for lifting the excommunication of Williamson and the other three bishops. He wrote of an *Amtsfehler*, a mistake in the exercise of the papal office, which in the light of canon law should be considered invalid. By way of an epilogue, Hünermann

---

[12] In 2012 Williamson would be expelled from the Society of St Pius V. He has illicitly ordained several more bishops, and leads a group that sets its face against any potential reconciliation with Rome.

quoted with deep dismay some reactionary and "uncatholic" items from the 1997 catechism of the Society of St Pius X. He prayed that God would be gracious to the Church, the Pope, and all the bishops.

(4) Fourth, in a 2007 *motu proprio* ("of one's own accord") or personal decree, largely as a gesture of reconciliation with the Society of St Pius X and its sympathizers, Pope Benedict authorized a wider use of the 1962 Latin Missal or what is often inaccurately called "the Tridentine Missal." The Council of Trent (1545–63) called for liturgical reforms but did not produce any missal. St Pius V did so in 1570. That missal for the Latin rite subsequently underwent minor modifications, right down to the eve of Vatican II. For instance, in 1960 John XXIII removed from the Good Friday prayers a phrase about "the perfidious Jews."

After Vatican II, a revised, standard form for the Latin rite was issued as the *Roman Missal* of Pope Paul VI. Published in Latin in 1970, it was then translated into the vernacular for use in Catholic worship around the world. Normally priests celebrate the Eucharist in their own language. But they have every right, and need no official permission, to use the Latin text of the 1970 Missal whenever they judge this appropriate.

By his 2007 *motu proprio* Pope Benedict left Latin-rite Catholics confusingly divided by two missals, the pre-Vatican II, unrevised *Roman Missal* of 1962 and Paul VI's *Missal* of 1970. If the Pope had acted collegially and asked Latin-rite bishops around the world for their opinion, it seems quite clear that the majority, even a vast majority, would have spoken against reintroducing the 1962 *Missal* as a licit alternative to that of 1970.[13]

---

[13] On John Paul II's already making the unrevised Missal available but only under certain circumstances, see John Wilkins, in G. O'Collins, with J. Wilkins, *Lost*

(5) Fifth, at the start of Advent 2011, an English version of the 1970 *Missal*, a so-called "sacred vernacular" that hovers uneasily between Latin and English, was introduced. With John Wilkins, in *Lost in Translation* I told the ugly story of a fine English translation approved by all eleven conferences of English-speaking bishops, called the *1998 Missal*, being set aside by the Vatican without any discussion. A clunky, latinized version prepared by a B-class team of translators was imposed in 2011.

At the direction of Pope Benedict, the *2011 Missal* replaced "for you and for all" with "for you and for many" in the words the priest says at Mass over the chalice when consecrating the wine. In a letter to the German Bishops' Conference (April 24, 2012), the Pope outlined his reasons for wanting the switch back to "for many." Central to his argument was a text about the Suffering Servant found in Isaiah 52: 13–53: 12). Benedict alleged that a previous scholarly agreement that "the many" (for whom the Servant suffers) means "all" had collapsed. It was news to exegetes that their consensus about the Hebrew text meaning "for all" had disappeared. What had happened was that the Pope no longer accepted their consensus.

Two Shining Features

Some shadows stretch over the pontificate of Benedict XVI. But two shining features should not be forgotten. From the first weeks of his papacy, he impressed the Roman public by homilies and addresses that were clear, brief, and thoroughly intelligible. Too often the words of John Paul II had been abstract and went right over the head of his audience. The change showed up right from the

---

in Translation: The English Language and the Catholic Mass (Collegeville, MN: Liturgical Press, 2017), 6–7.

Mass when Benedict was installed as pope in April 2005. At the end of his homily he declared with highly effective rhetoric: "If we let Christ into our lives, we lose nothing, nothing, absolutely nothing of what makes life free, beautiful and great."

In early 2013 Pope Benedict took the humble and courageous decision of resigning. He was worn out physically and mentally—not least by financial irregularities practised through the Vatican Bank and by the infighting of members of the Roman Curia. Careerism and cronyism, rather than a serious desire to serve the Pope, the Church and the world, characterized too many of those who belonged to the Vatican bureaucracy. The climax of the "mess" came with the trial and conviction of Pope Benedict's own butler, Paolo Gabriele. He had leaked confidential documents exposing power struggles in the Vatican.

When on March 13, 2013 a conclave of 115 cardinals elected Cardinal Jorge Bergoglio of Buenos Aires, the first Latin American to become pope, the choice reflected a widespread concern for a radical reform of the Curia and the desire for a pope without links to an establishment widely seen as dysfunctional and even corrupt. Future historians will, I believe, praise even more what Pope Benedict did in 2013 by standing down and opening the way for the election of Pope Francis.

Appendix: *Jesus of Nazareth* (volume one)

In the two-volume work that he began writing in 2003 and so two years before he was elected to the papacy, *Jesus of Nazareth* (Bloomsbury, 2007 and 2011), Benedict XVI showed once again a discomfort with biblical scholarship. At the same time, when publishing volume one he stipulated that "this book" was "in no way an exercise" of his official magisterium but "solely" a testimony to "his personal search for the face of the Lord." Through his position as head of the Catholic Church, the Pope seized the opportunity to spread around the world the good news that, in the person of Jesus of Nazareth, the Son of God has come among us and shares with us abundant life here and hereafter.

Even though Benedict began writing *Jesus of Nazareth* two years before he became pope, some sections of volume one read like beautifully crafted biblical homilies that had been preached and polished over many years. This is how the three chapters in which he presented the Lord's Prayer, the parables, and principal images in John's Gospel (water, vine and wine, bread, and shepherd) strike me. They read like the products of long study, prayerful meditation, and preaching. Whatever their precise origin, however, these chapters prompt a more profound preaching of several major themes in any portrait of Jesus, as well as a richer personal reading of the Gospels.

After eloquent pages on the seven petitions of the "Our Father," the Pope highlighted ways in which three parables, the Good Samaritan, the Prodigal Son (which he more accurately called the Parable of the Two Brothers and the Merciful Father), and the Rich Man and Lazarus show how "divine light shines through in the things of the world." They convey a knowledge of God "that makes demands on us." Over and over again, Benedict illustrated "the topical relevance" of the parables. He transposed, for instance, the Parable of the Good Samaritan into the dimensions of the world scene, recognizing how the people of Africa, in particular, have been "robbed and plundered" by a cynical "world without God in which all that counts are power and profit."

Contemporary, recent, and ancient biblical scholars and other authors enter the bibliography and the text itself. The long chapter about the Sermon on the Mount moves through the beatitudes to discuss with Rabbi Jacob Neusner the identity of Jesus as being himself the new Law. The beatitudes not only synthesize the program of God's kingdom but also give us a self-portrait of Jesus. Behind preaching purity of heart, the search for justice, and the rest, we find the uniquely authoritative claims of the Preacher himself. Summarizing the Sermon on the Mount for his Jewish dialogue-partner, the Pope concluded: Jesus "has brought the God of Israel to the nations, so that all the nations now pray to him and recognize Israel's Scriptures as the word of the living God. He has brought the gift of universality which was the one, great, definitive promise to Israel and the world." This "faith in the one God of Abraham, Isaac, and Jacob, extended now in Jesus' new family to all the nations," is the supreme "fruit of Jesus' work."

This book was shaped by the conviction that we can truly know Jesus through the Gospels and that in him we see the human face of God. Benedict argued that lesser portraits of Jesus as, for instance, merely a wandering prophet or a reforming rabbi, do not do justice to the historical evidence. They fail to explain why the relatively harmless figure they portray could be condemned to crucifixion and then have an enormous and lasting impact on millions of people. Benedict's book had an apologetic purpose, alongside its pastoral and spiritual message. Only God can demand of us what Jesus asks. The divine identity of Jesus is no optional extra.

Pope Benedict asked for "goodwill" from his readers, but added: "everyone is free to contradict me." Contradicting him would be unjustified, but some quibbles are in order. First, I emphatically agree that our historical knowledge of Jesus is indispensable, above all because God has persistently acted in human history and in Jesus has personally entered our history. Right down to *Rethinking Fundamental Theology*,[14] I have repeatedly argued that historical knowledge belongs essentially to Christian faith. I also agree that *some* biblical scholars have produced "the impression that we have very little certain knowledge of Jesus." But only some. Benedict should have acknowledged the work of such experts as Richard Bauckham, Raymond Brown, Richard Burridge, Brendan Byrne, James Dunn, Joseph Fitzmyer, Daniel Harrington, Richard Hays, Luke Timothy Johnson, Craig Keener, Dorothy Lee, Ulrich Luz, Joel Marcus, John Meier, Frank Moloney, Pheme Perkins, Sandra Schneiders, and Bishop Tom Wright—to name only some who do not give that impression. They encourage us to join the former pope in "trusting the Gospels," because we hear in and through the Gospel texts the reliable testimony of eyewitnesses and their associates.

Second, apropos of the liturgy, Benedict expressed his deep concern that "modern liturgists want to dismiss" the "social function of Sunday as a Constantinian aberration." Evidently he had read or heard of one or two liturgical scholars who maintain that Emperor Constantine made a mistake in March 321 by declaring Sunday a day of rest from work. But so far in my own life I have never come across a single liturgist who defends such a misguided view.

Third, it is important to be reminded of the way in which Eastern Christians have deepened our understanding of Jesus' baptism. But I wonder what they would think of this account of what happened at the river Jordan: "Jesus loaded the burden of all mankind's guilt upon his shoulders, and bore it down into the depths of the Jordan." More historically minded Western Christians might wonder about any texts of the Gospels supporting this view of what Jesus consciously

---

[14] Oxford: Oxford University Press, 2011.

did before entering the Jordan. What Benedict wrote looks like a devout but unjustified claim.

Despite such quibbles, we should admit that, at least in volume one, *Jesus of Nazareth* achieved its central purpose by showing a wider public how the divine Sonship of Jesus was "the source from which his action and teaching and suffering sprang." The book was a moving testimony to what Jesus meant to Joseph Ratzinger, who came to publish this work as Pope Benedict XVI.

Part II: Family

5
Patrick Francis ("Frank") O'Collins (1893–1961)

My father, Patrick Francis O'Collins, was born in Port Melbourne (Victoria, Australia) on October 28, 1893 in the midst of a general economic depression. That year governments slashed expenditure, banks closed their doors, and wanton land expenditure plus exuberant building programs brought ruin to many Victorian families. "Marvellous Melbourne" lost its leadership to Sydney. But the crash of '93 hardly touched my grandparents: Pat who had a lifelong job at the local gasworks, and Ellen who supplemented their income by running a small herd of dairy cattle and selling their milk. In their working-class home, they now enjoyed three sons, and would have two more sons and three daughters. All eight of their children were born at home. Two of the daughters (Mollie and Alice) became nuns and three of the sons (Will, Jim, and Gerald) priests. Jim went on to become a bishop, first of Geraldton (Western Australia) and then of Ballarat (Victoria).

My father was a heavily built man, close to six feet tall, with black hair and a tooth-brush moustache. His strength, correct bearing, and careful courtesy suggested an officer. At times he was known as "Captain," the final rank he held after serving in France with the 38th battalion of the Australian Imperial Force (A.I.F.) (1917–18) and with the Indian Army in the Punjab Province (1919). But later he was simply known as Frank or "P. F." O'Collins.

The first thing I can recall him saying was "cowards die many times." He was encouraging me not to be afraid of the dark and, especially, of those mysterious shadows and rustling shapes which I could see under the trees that rose to the south of our home, Rock Lodge.[15] He battled sickness (heart attacks and cancer), business problems, and other challenges with a fearlessness that made him stand tall among us like the big gum tree which divided our view to the north across Port Phillip Bay toward Melbourne. He stood there creating our landscape. He assured his six children that he kept a revolver in a secret cupboard. Long after I ceased to think of this gun as our defence weapon against a marauding world, I believed in this secret cupboard which now housed valuable documents, or so I thought.

Father was an exuberant, warmly affectionate man. When I grew up and mixed in wider society, I found it odd that other sons did not kiss their fathers but greeted them with a handshake. Very occasionally he spanked me or my younger brothers (Jim and Glynn) with a soft old slipper. I can still see the slipper although I cannot recall any particular occasions of punishment. What I do recall are times I rolled around the living room floor in rages, started a fire in grounds of our home by playing with matches,

---

[15] Father chose the name to recall Rock Lodge, the home of his mother on the banks of the River Shannon, from which she emigrated from Ireland to Australia in 1887.

seriously hurt Jim in a thoughtless accident, and did other things for which he might have thrashed me but never did.

He was extraordinarily controlled for such a vigorous man. He imposed few rules. We were forbidden to approach the large dam that lay to the west of our house or to lift the cover on an underground tank that flanked our front drive and supplied us with drinking water. When we three boys were supplied with bicycles, we were told not to ride them at night time. We were allowed to fire rifles and even two pistols, a Beretta and Luger, brought back from the North African campaign by Jim Peters (who was to marry my elder sister Moira). But Father insisted: "Never point a gun at anyone, even if you think it's not loaded."

My parents wanted their children to be rooted in the land, and for seven or eight years ran a poultry farm. Father looked on farming work as part of our education. With my younger brothers, I milked cows, separated the cream, made butter, fed the chickens, collected the eggs, killed and dressed the poultry, took our Jersey cows three miles away to be serviced by the local bull, cared for our ponies, collected fruit from the orchard, trapped rabbits, and occasionally grew vegetables. When we left for boarding school, Father had sold the cows and chickens, but kept the ponies for years. They became the delight of his granddaughters, who came for weekends

"Talk with the visitors" was a rule that prepared his three daughters (Moira, Dympna, and Maev) and three sons for life. A steady stream of visitors enriched life in our country home thirty miles down Port Phillip Bay from Melbourne. Along with his legal practice in the city, Father also moved into the cinema business, He was part owner of the Empire Theatre Brunswick, the Plaza Theatre Coburg, and a director of Gaiety Theatres which leased the King's Theatre in the

Central Business District of Melbourne. He built the Astor Theatre, St Kilda, in the Art Deco style that flourished in the 1930s. It now enjoys a heritage rating. People turned up at Rock Lodge from the movie theatre business. They must have accounted for one exotic group who came to visit in 1940. Members of the Bolshoi Ballet that had been stranded in Australia by the outbreak of World War II, a troupe of Russian ballerinas arrived wearing white furs and carrying Pekinese dogs. They danced across our front lawn like a flock of warm, exotic seagulls.

Father provided his children with informal educational opportunities galore through the wide variety of Australian and foreign visitors. We brought them drinks, stopped to chat, and sat with them at table. One was Hartley Grattan, a left-wing academic and leading American authority on Australian history and scholar. Over dinner one evening, Grattan began to explain how to stage a Communist revolution, but pulled himself up short with a plea to another guest, Sir Herbert Gepp: "stop me, Sir Herbert."[16] When they were together in Sydney and crossing the harbour by ferry, Father engaged Grattan in a debate over our human nature and destiny, tossed a coin for his immortal soul, and won. Grattan, who spent the last years of his life in Texas, left instructions in his will for his ashes to be scattered over Sydney harbour.

Father encouraged his guests to help with our education. Sir Edward McTiernan, a portly Labor politician who was appointed to the High Court of Australia in 1930, became its longest serving judge, and finally retired in 1976. He came close to marrying one of my Mother's sisters. With my Father's encouragement, McTiernan

---

[16] A mining industrialist and public servant, Gepp had strong American ties and used his influence to improve conditions for workers in Broken Hill and elsewhere. The *Australian Dictionary of Biography*, 18 vols (Melbourne: Melbourne University Press, 1966–2012) contains excellent entries on Gepp and Grattan.

regularly asked me to read him the speeches of Edmund Burke, a notable Whig politician (1729–97). Eventually I had to recite for him by heart Burke's famous Speech to the Electors of Bristol, delivered on November 3, 1774 and defending the independence of conscience for members of parliament.

With the arrival of American marines in the mid-years of World War II, Father's hospitality enjoyed a new outlet. Shortly after the bombing of Pearl Harbour in December 1941, he sighted two American army officers in the lounge of the Menzies Hotel, Melbourne, and strolled over to greet them. Delighted by their southern charm, he asked: "Are all American servicemen like you?" One of them warned with a laugh, "Just wait for the marines!" In late 1942 the Seventh Marine Regiment was withdrawn from fighting in the Solomon Islands, and arrived for rest and recreation at a camp in Mt Martha, about twelve miles south of our home on the Mornington peninsula. Father sought out Colonel Herman Henry Hanneken, who brought a group of his junior officers for parties at our home.

My eldest sister Moira has just finished her schooling at the Sacred Heart convent in Melbourne. She mustered her friends to help in the entertainment. They fluttered around our house, all legs and laughter—lovely, elusive creatures from a grown-up world. Josie Filippini, the daughter of Contessa Filippini who taught Italian at Moira's school, charmed Hanneken with her sparkling beauty. A permanent marine, he was friendly, fatherly, and steely—clearly a different stamp of soldier from the cheerful young officers he brought with him. Momentarily, when they danced together, the tough fighter seemed softened by the innocent loveliness of a girl just out of convent school.

Some the marines Father welcomed to our home died later in battles at Cape Gloucester and Peleliu. A graduate of the legendary University of Notre Dame (South Bend, Indiana), Ed Kirby survived, became a lawyer in New Jersey, and remained in lasting contact with my family. For five years I was to enjoy Thanksgiving Dinner at his home in Upper Montclair.

After Hanneken and his regiment moved back to the fighting, Father kept up his contacts with the camp and met General Lemuel C. Shepherd, Jr, then a brigadier general and later the 20th Commandant of the US Marine Corps.[17] At Shepherd's invitation, I lunched in a mess with the marines and enjoyed a ride out into Port Phillip Bay on an amphibious landing craft. Mrs Eleanor Roosevelt came to visit the camp. I stood by the roadside to wave to her as an official car whisked her by. Many years before any of us ever visited the United States, Father brought his six children into contact with dozens of Americans. He let us travel abroad before we ever left home.

Notable representatives from England made their way to Rock Lodge. When in January 1935 the "10,000 Boy Scouts' Jamboree" was held in the bush just north of our home, Father and Mother entertained the Chief Scout (and founder of the modern scouting movement), Baron Baden-Powell. He came wearing the broad brimmed hat of the scouts and accompanied by a scouting party. Governor of Victoria from 1949 to 1963, Sir Reginald Dallas Brooks was the longest serving governor of that Australian state. Early in his tenure my parents hosted a garden party at Rock Lodge to let him meet informally church leaders and Catholic members of professional, business, and community groups.

---

[17] When he became commandant, Shepherd replied on February 25, 1952 to Father's letter of congratulation: "It was indeed a pleasure to have news of you again. I always remember your gracious hospitality to me during the period I served in the First Division at Mt Martha."

Father wanted us to grow up confident and ready to make our way anywhere. He told us stories of the months he spent at Magdalen College, when he was withdrawn from the frontline in France to take an officers' training course in Oxford. The Magdalen dons treated the cadets as normal undergraduates and kept up the usual formalities, including dinner with full silver. Bathtubs were still the rule at Magdalen. But the college agreed to install outside showers for the Australians. Father quickly struck up a friendship with Colonel Cox, an ex-Indian army officer and now commander of the 6th battalion cadets. One Sunday, Cox took him to dine with the English critic, Sir Walter Raleigh (1861–1922), and Raleigh's only daughter. One of Raleigh's sons was a prisoner of war in Germany, and had written to tell his father that he was being treated well, Colonel Cox objected: "It's wrong to praise the Germans." "One must tell the truth," retorted Raleigh. Six feet six tall and a fellow of Magdalen, Raleigh spoke enthusiastically of India, where he taught for two years at the beginning of his academic career. But Cox talked of the German threat in India and urged Father to join the Indian Army then and there. But Father felt obliged to return to his company in France. "All the same," he promised, "if I am alive in six months time, I will go to India." Six months to the day, the order came in July 1918 to proceed to the India Office in London. His appointment with the A.I.F. ended and he accepted a commission in the Indian Army.

A born teacher, Father gave his children a taste for England and its university life. It was no accident that I received my PhD at the University of Cambridge (1968) after becoming a research fellow of Pembroke College. He had shared with us the magic of Oxford and Cambridge. He also gave us a lasting love for the rich spirituality and culture of India—not least the poetry of the

Bengali poet Rabindrinath Tagore whom he heard lecture. It was Tagore that I quoted when sitting on the edge of the Trevi Fountain in Rome and making a film for an Australian television channel (1997). But the day Father joined his regiment in the Punjab Province, April 13, 1919, was a day of infamy for the British raj. Brigadier General Reginald Dyer ordered the fifty Gurkhas under this command to fire on unarmed citizens in Amritsar and killed at least 379 people. Dyer's troops were not under threat; the general aimed at intimidating people agitating for home rule in India. Then the third Anglo-Afghan War broke out on May 3, and Father moved to the area of fighting near the Khyber Pass. This war ended quickly with a peace treaty signed at Rawalpindi on August 8. At the end of September 1919, Father resigned his commission, left his regiment as captain, and, with wonderful photos, a marble chessboard, and other lasting memorabilia from India, sailed home to Melbourne.

I always remained astonished at the speed with which Father settled back into academic and civilian life. In the Melbourne University examinations at the end of 1919, he passed one or two subjects to complete his B.A. His two years of arts at the Melbourne University's Teachers College in 1913 and 1914 had left the degree unfinished. In 1920 he began his law studies and four years of residence at Newman College, the Catholic men's college within the University of Melbourne. After finishing his L.L.B. at the end of 1921, Father remained at Newman for two more years as resident law-tutor, and completed a Master of Law degree. In 1924, he joined a firm of Collins Street (at the heart of down town Melbourne) and quickly became a senior partner. That was the year he married my Mother.

Father wanted his three daughters (Moira, Dympna, and Maev) and three sons (myself, Jim, and Glynn) to grow up open to a wider world and free of narrow Catholic tribalism. Part of that training centered on Peninsula Country Golf Club, close to our home and presided over by Major General Harold Grimwade, who, during World War I, had skilfully commanded Australian artillery on the Western Front.[18] One of its leading personalities and players, Father won every competition at the club except the championship. The year he died (1961) his youngest son, Glynn, became club champion for the first (of thirteen) times.

The only piece of autobiographical material Father left in writing was an account of his first (and only?) hole-in-one in 1939. He entitled the story "Called to the bar."

"This story was given to the *Herald* by the club professional, Bill Clifford.[19] The facts are as follows. On Sunday March 12, Councillor Raymond Connelly holed out in one on the 12th hole. That evening Ray spent at our home. Next day, Monday 13 March, was Labour Day [a public holiday], with a four ball best ball to be played. In the morning I played with Norman Brookes; we were six up. As we came in, Stanley Bruce was on the putting green. He had arrived from London a few days earlier. He joined us for a spot. I suggested that he play with Norman in the afternoon against me and my partner. Ray was in the room and he agreed to make up the four. At the 12th, I mentioned that Ray had holed out in one and invited Norman 'to do the same.' He said that he had already done so on two occasions and promptly put his ball on the green. Bruce (known as 'Joe') was also invited 'to do the same' He said that he had never

---

[18] In his letters written from France during World War I, the Australian general John Monash showed how much he could rely on expert artillery support from Grimwade; see A. K. Macdougall (ed.), *War Letters of General Monash* (Melbourne: Angus and Robertson, 2015), 127–28, 130.

[19] A daily paper published in Melbourne, the *Herald* was purchased in 1987 by Rupert Murdoch. and renamed the *Herald Sun*.

holed in one nor seen anyone get an ace. He then put his ball on the green. I then said to Ray: 'Come on. Show us that yesterday's one was not a fluke.' He put his ball into the timber, where it remains today. Ray then said to me: 'You are having a lot to say. I did it on the limit (24), and you are on two and have never had one. See what you can do today.' I then said: 'They say that you throw it down like this, and you hit it in like that.' To our amazement, the ball dropped and rolled an inch or two into the cup. Ray and I went on to win the competition eight up. But we would not have done so if Bruce had not missed at least four putts of less than two feet. Today the four players are Lord Bruce of Melbourne, Sir Norman Brookes, the late Sir Raymond Connelly (former Lord Mayor of Melbourne), and the Knight of Rock Lodge."

Bruce was Prime Minister of Australia (1925–29) and Australian High Commissioner in London (1933–45). Connelly helped secure the 1956 Olympic Games for Melbourne, but died before they were held. Brookes had been twice the men's singles champion at Wimbledon (1907 and 1914), being the first non-Briton and first left-hander to do so.

I was not with my father on the occasion of his sensational hole in one. But later I often caddied or carried his golf clubs for him. A game that remains in my memory was one with Norman Brookes and Gerald Patterson. Like Brookes, Patterson had been twice the men's singles champion at Wimbledon and a very successful Davis Cup player. Where Brookes was nicknamed "the Wizard," Patterson was known as "the Human Catapult" for his powerful serves that even top players had trouble in returning. The fourth in that golf match was Harry Hopman, a good tennis player who was on the way to becoming a highly successful Davis Cup coach. A nephew of the legendary soprano Dame Nellie Melba (1861–1931) and

Brookes's former partner in doubles, Patterson thumped his drive as hard as he was supposed to have hit his serve. Courteous and precise, Brookes carefully directed his ball down the middle of the fairway. It was tiring work following the game around the course for three hours or more, but encouraging, since Father won far more often than he lost.

Father had hoped that I might follow him in the legal profession. But he accepted my decision to enter the Society of Jesus, and took pleasure at my academic success. He attended the ceremony in 1958 when I received the gold medal in classics from the University of Melbourne. But heart failure was draining the power from his thick frame. I had begun theological studies at Canisius College, Pymble (a suburb of Sydney) when the dreaded phone call came one Saturday morning in February 1961, Father had been rushed to the Mercy Hospital, East Melbourne, and was dying. That afternoon I flew from Sydney to Melbourne, my first airplane flight as a Jesuit.

When I reached the hospital room, Father's eyes flicked towards me in recognition, but he could say nothing. The next day he was in a deep coma. His breath came in great irregular gasps. We knelt around the bed to say the rosary. At three o'clock in the afternoon Father's breathing stopped. The room was silent, except for the quiet hiss of the oxygen escaping from the mask. After some minutes Mother said, "I would like to go to the chapel." Through the sun-drenched afternoon I took her across to the courtyard to the hospital chapel and prayed. "I want to see him again for a moment," she said. We went back to the room. She pressed a kiss on his forehead and left.

Two nuns, old friends who had nursed Father during several stays in the Mercy Hospital, took me to a room where I phoned Campion

Hall, a Jesuit house of studies. It was immensely cheering when a group of scholastics, the Jesuit name for our seminarians, instantly agreed to sing the requiem Mass to be celebrated in St Patrick's Cathedral. I laid down the phone and wept—the first tears I had shed since childhood. "We all loved him so much," I murmured to the sisters as the tears poured down my cheeks. Life suddenly seemed strangely lonely. The rock on which I stood had been swept away.

An officer and a gentleman, Father was a man of unfailing hospitality and openness to all, He felt very much at home in all manner of institutions: his family, the Catholic Church, his high school, the army, Newman College (on whose council he served until his death), the legal establishment of Melbourne, Peninsula Country Golf Club, and other clubs. His three years at the Melbourne Continuation School (renamed the Melbourne High School in 1911) set the pattern for his life.

After winning a scholarship to study there from 1910 to 1912, Father won the Rix Prize in 1911 and was elected by staff and students head prefect for 1912. The Rix Prize went to the boy, "who in the judgment of the staff has shown the best character, asserted the strongest influence for good, and made the greatest progress in his studies." The years at this school gave Father the opportunity to establish lasting friendships beyond Irish-Catholic circles, to register high academic achievements, and prove successful as leader and sportsman.

His most notable friendship across the frontiers of creed and culture grew with the headmaster himself, Joseph Hocking. Father's obituary in the 1961 issue of the school magazine recalled that Hocking's narrow religious outlook opposed anything and everything Roman Catholic. It was between an essentially Catholic schoolboy and an equally devout Protestant headmaster that an affinity developed. During the dark days of World War I, they corresponded as friends and some of those letters were published in the school magazine of the day.

Father taught me many things, not least never to indulge self-pity. During a visit to Sydney in 1959, he had fallen ill, but he brushed that aside when I saw him a few months later. He preferred to describe with relish a reception given at a Sydney club by Alfred Hitchcock, then an established director of "thrillers." A hearse stood outside the club when Mother and Father arrived. Lighting was subdued. The waitresses were dressed in black, like widows. A number of guests spotted the hearse and drove away at once, thinking that someone had died in the club. Those who came in to the reception stood around drinking, chatting nervously, and being discreetly filmed by Hitchcock. They jumped and screamed when—at a prearranged moment—a waitress suddenly let a large tray of glasses crash to the floor.

Shortly after Easter 1993, Father's words about holding a chair at table only for ladies and never for gentlemen rang in my ears when I lunched with Pope John Paul II. The pope had brought together a team of scholars to discuss with him the nature of redemption one late morning, and we were invited to stay on for a meal in the papal apartments. I found my place at the right hand of the pope. Remembering what Father had said, I did not take the pope's chair when he was sitting down.

Our conversation covered a range of theological subjects. A lull came and I thought of Father's sporting passion. Since the lunch took place only a few weeks after Easter, I remarked: "Holiness, you had competition this last Easter Sunday from a German golfer, Bernard Langer. On Easter Sunday, he too announced the good news of Christ's resurrection to millions of people, but he did that from the 18th green after winning a major golf tournament." "Langer? Golf?," the pope knew nothing of all that. So I had to explain that in the previous year, on his last putt, Langer had lost the Ryder Cup for the European team. The following spring he had, so to speak, come back from the dead to win the Master's at Atlanta (Georgia). As he put on the green jacket, he told the public of his joy in winning on Easter Sunday, "the greatest day of the year, the day when Jesus rose from the dead." I was only sorry that Father was long dead. I could not share with him what was said at the papal table.

6
Joan O'Collins
(1899–1977)

Mother was the eldest of seven surviving children born to Patrick ("Paddy") and Abigail McMahon Glynn. An Irish barrister, Paddy reached Melbourne, Australia, in October 1880 with a letter of introduction to Sir Redmond Barry, like my grandfather a graduate of Trinity College Dublin. A judge of the Supreme Court of Victoria since 1853, at sixty-seven Barry was still an active, though portly, man. At the time of Paddy's arrival, he was out of town and returned to try the notorious outlaw Ned Kelly on October 28 and 29. On the second day of the trial grandfather lunched with Barry, and returned to court to hear the sentence of death passed and Kelly's famous words to the judge: "I will see you there when I go." The following month, twelve days after Kelly's execution, Barry died unexpectedly—unexpectedly for the general public but not for his doctors.

Barry annoyed grandfather by telling him to go home at once to Ireland, as migrant barristers stood very little chance of success. In the event, Paddy failed to find a niche in Melbourne, and moved to Adelaide, South Australia, where he established himself in his profession, and also moved beyond law to become a politician, renowned for his humour, eloquence, and learning.

He was a leading figure in the Federal Convention (1897–98), and, after the six Australian states federated, was elected to the House of Representatives in 1901. He became a minister in three Commonwealth governments. His nineteen years as a member made him the last of the "Founding Fathers" to remain in the national parliament.

During the 1897 Federal Convention in Sydney, grandfather dashed down to Melbourne, married Abigail Dynon, and, to the astonishment of the other delegates, returned at once with his bride to continue work on the Australian constitution.[20] His most famous contribution was an amendment embodying a reference to God in the preamble ("Humbly relying on the blessing of almighty God"). In a brief speech he made before the amendment was passed without division, he proposed the amendment as "simple and unsectarian" and "expressive of the great elemental truth upon which all our

---

[20] His letter of September 7, 1897 proposing marriage to grandmother appears in B. Niall and J. Thompson (eds), *Australian Letters* (Melbourne: Oxford University Press, 1998), 120–21.

creeds are based." "We cannot," he argued, "at the moment of entering into a union so full of the possibilities of good and evil, refuse to give expression to the central fact of all our faiths."[21]

Grandfather died a few months after I was born on June 2, 1931. But he remained a living presence, as our home housed his magnificent private library, diaries, and his other private papers. Mother remained intensely proud of what he had achieved. Among other things, she inherited from him a deep love of the classics, and would make sure that I began studying Latin and ancient Greek at the age of twelve. She was delighted when I published grandfather's biography and then a volume of his letters.

As a child, Mother had bonded in a special way with her father, He would provide all the bedtime stories she wanted, reading to her from the *Arabian Nights* and, even when she was quite young, from Edgar Allan Poe and Shakespeare. He loved her bright, considerate nature and felt her influence. One night, as he waited for her to climb into bed, he was making some notes from a recent book which aimed to explain the universe wholly in terms of an endless, mechanical round of evolution and devolution. "Yet," he wrote in his diary for November 2, 1907, "how much more beautiful and reassuring is the contemplation at this moment of a child saying to herself her evening prayers."

Mother grew up in North Adelaide, suffered from various illnesses, including a bout of rheumatic fever, but enjoyed an excellent education in a local school run by Dominican sisters. They gave her a lifelong passion for reading.

---

[21] I published a life of grandfather, *Patrick McMahon Glynn: A Founder of Australian Federation* (Melbourne: Melbourne University Press, 1965), and some of his letters, *Patrick McMahon Glynn: Letters to His Family (1874–1927)* (Melbourne: Polding Press, 1974).

Mother and Father met at a tea party in Newman College (University of Melbourne) in September 1920 when she came across to Melbourne for a holiday. A few days later they were together at the Newman Society Ball, where Father secured almost every dance with her. He wrote to her after her return to Adelaide, but she decided not to answer the letter when one of her sisters remarked: "Oh! Frank O'Collins, he's a real ladies man!" But he was forcefully reminded of Mother in September 1921, when he dined with her father at Newman high table. Father met Mother again during her visit to Melbourne in late 1922. Within a week they became engaged. In the overnight train going back to Adelaide, she kept switching on the light in her sleeper to look at the engagement ring and re-assure herself that it was not all a dream.

But, before they could marry, Father needed to establish himself in his legal career. A few months later Mother left for a year in Europe with her sister Dympna. When staying in Paris, Mother visited the Madeleine (a church dedicated to St Mary Magdalene) and prayed that she might have a son who would become a priest. (That prayer prompted me many years later into always giving Mary Magdalene a good theological press.[22]) In Rome, Mother and her sister were entertained by Father's brother Jim, who had been ordained a priest on Christmas Eve 1922 and would leave for Australia six months later. In November 1923. Mother and Dympna were in Munich for Adolf Hitler's abortive Beer Hall Putsch and witnessed some disturbances in the streets. But a policeman assured the two young women, "Don't get worried. It's only a silly idiot who won't come to anything."

Finally, on May 28, 1924, my parents were married at St

---

[22] See the article I wrote with Daniel Kendall, "Mary Magdalene as Major Witness to Jesus' Resurrection," *Theological Studies* 48 (1987), 631–46.

Lawrence's church, North Adelaide, with two of Father's brothers (Jim and Will) celebrating the wedding. Initially they lived in St Kilda and Brighton, two pretty, bay-side suburbs of Melbourne. Five years later Father visited Frankston to check a block of land for a client. Three miles beyond the township, on the slopes of Mt Eliza, he noticed a 24-acre farm with a "For Sale" signed posted. He walked in and at once fell in love with the view that stretched across Port Phillip Bay to the city of Melbourne and the surrounding plains and mountains. He phoned Mother to come down immediately. That same day he bought the whole property for £1,200. They had wanted a place in the country, and Father's discovery exceeded their dreams. The house they built, Rock Lodge, became the home in which I grew up.

Mother was delicately beautiful, of middle size, and possessed a pleasant, gentle voice. After her hair turned prematurely grey, she dyed it light brown. She was absolutely dedicated to my Father, very rarely opposed him, and when necessary achieved her objectives through indirect means rather than direct discussion. Eventually the large dam behind our house was turned into a 40,000 gallon, underground tank to supplement our water supply and enable Mother to improve the large garden. Father always thought the scheme was his, and boasted that the concrete tank could serve as a shelter in time of nuclear war. But we children knew that Mother was the real author of the scheme.

She worried about Father's skin cancer, for which he had a serious operation on his neck and one shoulder in 1941 and, subsequently, radium treatment for various "spots" on his face. Around that time we occasionally gathered for a family rosary. After the prayers, Mother would dab Father's face with water from the Blessed Virgin Mary's shrine in Lourdes. She never seemed totally robust herself. A miscarriage cast heavy gloom over one childhood Christmas. She had five or six miscarriages and at least one still-born child. Yet she helped to teach us tennis and golf, and through the 1930s worked on our poultry farm. If she was restrained in showing physical affection, we all picked up her language of "pet," "darling," and other endearments.

We felt totally certain of our parents' love. They left the six of us surprisingly free to follow our own initiatives, supported us in what we attempted, and tried discreetly to provide conditions for growth toward human and Christian maturity. I can recall very few occasions when we were forced to do something. Once Mother stood beside a ladder and made me climb it to overcome my fear of heights.

In 1936, my Father's beloved Newman College participated in "The Pageant of History —and All That," which raised money to build the Union House at Melbourne University. In the pageant Mother portrayed Mary Queen of Scots, with her first two daughters, Moira and Dympna, accompanying her as "ladies in waiting." A regal photo of Mother hung proudly in our home.

After I left home in 1950 to join the Society of Jesus, I saw my parents only spasmodically. During some years I was teaching or studying interstate—in Perth (Western Australia) or in Pymble, a northern suburb of Sydney. Father had died two years earlier but Mother was proudly there in January 1963 when Bishop James O'Collins ordained me in his cathedral at Ballarat, a country city in the State of Victoria. After the ninety-minute Mass and ordination ceremony, I came out of the sacristy to give my blessing. A newly ordained priest made a sign of the cross over the head of men and on the shoulders of women (who still often wore hats in church), and allowed them to kiss both his hands. My Mother knelt there, the first in line to receive my blessing (in Latin). I felt so overwhelmed by love and gratitude toward her that I could scarcely pronounce the words of blessing.

The following year I left for Münster in Germany to complete my final year of training as a Jesuit. In June 1965, on her first trip overseas since 1923, Mother travelled alone to Europe. When she moved north from Italy, I hired a car in Cologne and drove south to meet her in Heidelberg. I felt impatient to start my doctoral studies at the University of Cambridge, but became quickly infected with Mother's sheer delight at the beauty of Europe.

We marvelled at the great Romanesque cathedral in Speyer, tracked down the original Liebfrauenmilch vineyard near Worms, admired Balthasar Neumann's altar in the Worms cathedral, and paid our respects to the Luther monument. At a meeting with the civil and religious authorities in Worms, he was challenged about his writings and is supposed to have said, "this is my position. I cannot shift (*hier stehe ich. Ich kann nicht anders*"). Naturally we explored romantic Heidelberg thoroughly. I pointed out to Mother the full title of its Catholic parish priest: Stadtpfarrer Monsignor Professor Doktor Richard Hauser.

From Heidelberg we drove up the Neckar to Tübingen, where we stayed in the Hotel Lamm, right on the ancient market place. For us it was love at first sight, when we glimpsed the fifteenth-century townhall festooned with flowers. We found in Tübingen what we had looked for in Heidelberg: the unspoiled beauty of a medieval, university town. At the Lamm a waitress suggested to us their kangaroo-tail soup. When we chose something else, she smilingly agreed: "Of course, we don't take our native dishes when we are abroad." Mother and I did not have the heart to tell her that, unlike many Germans, we had never in our life tasted this soup.

We made a refreshing stop at the Benedictine monastery of Maria Laach, near Cologne. Mother did not know what to praise more highly: the beauty of the liturgy or the unsophisticated comfort of the hotel. As we left, she assured me: "it's been a real cure for body and soul." We crossed to England after a fortnight of constant travel that gratified Mother and satisfied my academic hunger by visiting the universities of Heidelberg, Tübingen, Freiburg im Breisgau, Strasbourg, Cologne, and Louvain. Mother was useless in reading road maps, but German roads were splendidly signposted. She had an insatiable interest in the monuments and history of the places we visited. With her love for me little short of adoration, she delighted in having me to herself for the first time since I was born.

After five days in London we flew on to Dublin and set off quickly to County Limerick. Father's relatives on his mother's (Fitzgerald) side greeted us with enthusiastic affection. Sunlight poured down on the wide Shannon estuary. The hills of Clare beckoned from across those shining waters. The scenery and the occasion blended to convey a deep sense of peace.

From Limerick we drove north to Gort, the town where Mother's father, Paddy Glynn, was born and grew up. It lies deep in the west of Ireland. The Blackwater River, which flows through Gort, runs underground for much of its course, emerges here and there in holes, and empties at last into Coole Lake. This is the river celebrated by W. B. Yeats in his poem "Coole Park and Ballylee, 1931," written from his Norman tower on the river banks, Ballylee, more than fifty years after my grandfather left for Australia.

We visited grandfather's home (now a bank), his school (where he had been taught by a nun who nursed with Florence Nightingale in the Crimea), the church where he worshipped, and the cemetery where his parents and ancestors lay buried. With scrubbing brush, washing soda, and a bucket of hot water, we attacked their tombstones. The moss and lichen fell away to reveal the names of Paddy Glynn's forebears. Mother had visited Dublin in 1923, met some of her father's family, but did not head across the country to Gort. Being able to visit the place from which Paddy Gynn came pacified a deep need to hunt down his origins and settle her historical roots. There were no relatives still living in Gort, but she now knew at first hand the home of her beloved father.

The parish priest of Gort, who had met uncle Jim and uncle Gerald during his studies at the Irish College in Rome, startled Mother by asking, "Now, what's all this about the ecumenical movement?" Then we learned that his entire parish contained only one non-Catholic family. But the townspeople remembered with gratitude that during "the Troubles" the Church of Ireland minister rushed out to prevent British troops from carrying out their threat to burn Gort to the ground.

Mother and I flew back to London. Before she left for Australia, we took afternoon tea at a legendary meeting place, Simpson's on the Strand. It was over forty years since Mother had last taken tea there—on her first trip to Europe in 1923. Something she said prompted the courteous English waiter into thinking that she was born in the United Kingdom and had moved elsewhere. He remarked: "Madam, I gather you have lived abroad for some time." Mother's sense of happy nostalgia was complete.

In October 1965 I began doctoral studies at the University of Cambridge, and had completed two years when I went to Paris to take my final vows as a Jesuit on August 15, 1967. Most of the other eight Jesuits who took these vows with me had made a special trip to Paris, so that they could do so in a chapel of Montmartre, where the founder of our religious order, St Ignatius of Loyola, and his first companions took vows together on August 15, 1534. The simplicity of the occasion struck me, as one after another we vowed ourselves that morning to remain Jesuits for life.

Mother and my third sister Maev arrived in Paris later that day. Maev had flown straight from Australia, but Mother had been visiting Iceland and wanted to tell us all about growing potatoes in that country. We hired a car and set off on a trip for eleven days that took us north through Verdun to Trier, south through Colmar to Provence, and then back to Paris by way of the Loire valley and Chartres. It was a particularly happy holiday together. Mother loved "la belle France," and she revelled in the fact that, unlike Maev and myself, she spoke passable French and could take charge of purchases and bookings.

At Verdun, a cemetery in which 150,000 French soldiers lie buried, remnants of forts and trenches, and acres of land poisoned by incessant shelling recalled the carnage of the First World War. But Mother never expressed a wish to visit a stretch of the front where Father had fought with the 38th battalion of the A.I.F. and in April 1918 had seen the end of the legendary German ace, Baron Manfred von Richthofen. When two Lewis gunners providing cover for Australian artillery brought the Red Baron down,[23] Father and other soldiers rushed to the scene to secure a souvenir. In 1919 he brought home a large piece of von Richthofen's plane. To his annoyance, Mother gave the souvenir away during a metal drive

---

[23] See A. K. Macdougall (ed.), *War Letters of Sir John Monash* (Melbourne: Angus and Robertson, 2013).

in the Second World War. I often wondered whether she avoided visiting the scene of the Red Baron's death in case Maev or I raised the sensitive topic of the lost souvenir. Or was it rather a reluctance to see where Father had engaged in brutal fighting and lost some dear friends?

The sunlight blazing down on vineyards and broken columns made Provence sheer joy. Out of respect for the church councils held there, I suggested Orange as our base for visiting Arles, Avignon, Nimes, and Châteauneuf-du-Pape. We were all glad to arrive alive. On a deserted "autoroute" heading down to Orange, Maev was driving at nearly ninety miles an hour. A Chevrolet passed us, pulled fifty yards clear, and blew a front tire. Somehow the Dutch driver kept his twisting, spinning car on the road, while Maev managed to slide our Peugeot past.

Over in England, an American friend provided me with three tickets for a bloodthirsty and memorable performance of *Macbeth* starring Paul Scofield. Maev and I learned our lesson that evening. We had joked about Mother's habit of falling into conversation with strangers, kept our distance when she looked as if she was about to pounce, and made up a description to be circulated to the European police: "Grey-haired lady, aged sixty-seven, height five feet four inches, will talk on sight." That evening at Stratford on Avon, she joined us after the interval to report with glee a long conversation with a descendant of Sarah Siddons (1755–1831), a famous actress known for playing Lady Macbeth.

After settling in Rome from August 1974 as a full-time professor at the Gregorian University, every week or so Mother and I shared news by letter. I still returned to Australia for visits during the northern hemisphere summer. The summer of 1975, for instance, took me to lecture at a summer school in Vermont (a week) and in New Zealand (three weeks)— at Holy Cross Seminary in Mosgiel, a small town about ten miles out of Dunedin in the South Island of New Zealand. The homestead, around which the town grew, had belonged to a great nephew of the Scottish poet Robert Burns and took its name from Burns's farm,"Mossgiel." Somehow the second "s" got lost on the journey out from Scotland. On July 20 I wrote a long letter to my Mother.

"Time is whistling by here in the South Island. Unkind critics (noting the drift to the North Island which set in when the gold rush days ended) remark: 'Will the last person in the South Island please switch off the lights.' That's as bad as the story of the pilot telling the passengers: 'You are now approaching Auckland, New Zealand. Please put your watches back thirty years.' All very unfair. People have been extraordinarily hospitable to me, and I appreciate the sense of dialogue which seems to operate at all levels.

Theologians swarm regularly to New Zealand. The great Brazilian archbishop Helder Camara will be here shortly, and a Dominican from Jerusalem, Jerry Murphy-O'Connor, is already here. I am due to meet Monsignor Ralph Brown from London's Westminster Archdiocese who refused to give me an imprimatur for my dogma book last year.[24] He is in New Zealand lecturing on marriage tribunals. What do you say to a man who has refused you an imprimatur? From his letters he seemed a pleasant person, but stuck with a highly conservative cardinal and archdiocese.

There are about thirty seminarians at Holy Cross, many of them with good Protestant-sounding names like Wynn Williams and Hay-McKenzie. One of the staff explained that this was because the girls

---

[24] *Has Dogma a Future?* (London: Darton, Longman & Todd, 1975).

stuck to their Catholic faith and passed it on to their sons although they sometimes married Protestants. On his mother's side Wynn-Williams is related to Father Damien of Molokai. [This nineteenth-century missionary to lepers on an island near Hawaii has since been canonized as Saint Joseph de Veuster.]"

Just before Christmas 1976 my brothers and sister sent me a ticket to fly home to Melbourne, as Mother was fading fast. Classes ended and I was to catch a flight the following day. A couple of Irish students decided to take me off to a *trattoria* where I had never been before. At the end of the meal our waiter cheerfully asked what we were going to do at Christmas. When I told him that I would be flying home to Australia, since "la Mamma sta molto male (my Mother is very sick)," his face turned serious and he kissed me on both cheeks. This stranger instantly became a brother when he found me facing a painful loss at the heart of my family life. Where else in the world would a waiter whom I had met for the first time express his concern with such spontaneous feeling? In March 1977, Mother was rushed to hospital and died. One of the memories that softened the pain was the impromptu kindness of that Italian waiter on a December evening a few months earlier.

7
Moira Peters
(1925–2017)

Her age set my eldest sister apart as an adult when I first became aware of her as a separate character. Small, red-haired, and energetic, Moira tackled study, singing, acting, and social life with practical and wise enthusiasm.

Growing Up and Launching a Family

Like many eldest daughters, Moira was the apple of her father's eye and she shared his love of learning. Educated by a governess at home in Rock Lodge, she read the classics in our large library. She treasured nineteenth-century novelists and the poetry of Wordsworth and Tennyson. Before the Second World War, she left to board at Sacre Coeur (Melbourne), where she became head girl, an outstanding student, and dux of the school. In the state examinations at the end of her final year (1942), she scored first class honours in English, History, Italian, and Japanese. She was awarded a Newman College scholarship; in English she was third in the State of Victoria; and she won the state exhibition in Japanese. These excellent results set a standard of achievement for her siblings. She took Japanese, because Mother and Father thought it would be useful to have one member of our family fluent in that language, just in case the Japanese succeeded in overrunning Australia.

Six years apart in age, Moira and I rode horses and played tennis and golf together. After dark one winter evening, Moira and I were alone at Rock Lodge when we heard noises coming from a shed halfway along our front drive. I grabbed an unloaded shotgun. Moira armed herself with a heavy iron bar, which we used as a poker for a huge, central fireplace in the sitting room. We crept close the shed and with shaky voices called out: "Who's there?" It was a truck driver making a late delivery of grain for our cows and chickens. We slipped our weapons behind some lavender bushes and tried to chat to the driver in normal voices.

With her red hair and vivacious beauty, Moira won hearts among the American officers her parents entertained during the Second World War. She planned to be a journalist and began studying Arts at the University of Melbourne. One day in December 1943, Father asked her to accompany by train from the city a friend of his, a major who had returned from the campaign in North Africa. Expecting that this friend would be an agreeable but middle-aged officer, she met instead a very handsome medical doctor, Jim Peters. He was thirty years of age, and Moira was only eighteen. For Moira it was love at first sight, but Jim took little notice of her for two years.

During his medical studies as a resident at Newman College (University of Melbourne), Jim had come to know Father quite well—not least through sporting successes. As an Australian

Rules footballer, Jim captained the Newman College team and once kicked eighteen goals in a match against Queen's College. A freshman blue in 1931, he played with the University Blacks and in 1935 captained them to a championship. He also captained the Victorian amateurs and an All-Australian representative team. As an outstanding player of the 1930s, he was inducted by the Victorian Amateur Football Association in 2007 as the first "legend" of the game.

When the World War II broke out, Jim enlisted and was posted to North Africa with the Sixth Division. He served with distinction at the Siege of Tobruk and the Battle of El Alamein, and was mentioned in despatches. In Tobruk he used to go around the perimeter in the morning and check how the soldiers were doing in the gun pits. For the mega-battle at El Alamein, he organized quicker and more efficient ways of helping the wounded. After the war ended in 1945, Jim left the army as a lieutenant-colonel and began specializing in urology. He became a resident medical officer at Royal Melbourne Hospital, set himself to complete his MS (master of surgery), and began taking Moira out. A great love affair blossomed, and Jim was to tell his children: "The best thing that I ever did was marry Mum."

On the morning of April 6, 1946, they were married in the chapel of his beloved Newman College. That afternoon Jim formally received his Master of Surgery. At the reception in the evening I was detailed to take care of the widow of a man who had made his fortune in gold mines. She was dripping with diamonds, kindly, and a bit vague. A week later the newly weds sailed for England.

Jim became a resident surgical officer at St James' Hospital (London) and set himself to secure his FRCS (Fellow of the Royal College of Surgeons). The highlight of their first week in London was watching the Victory March on June 6, 1946 from the balcony of Australia House in the Strand. It was a magnificent spectacle, bringing together service-men and -women from far-flung countries of the British Empire— truly the end of an era.

After their eldest child, Stewart, was born, Jim received his FRCS and left for the United States where he took post-graduate terms at the Mayo and Cleveland Clinics. Moira returned to Melbourne with Stewart and expecting a second child. Still a schoolboy at Xavier College, I felt slightly heroic declining an invitation to a party, so that I could be on hand the weekend Marion was born in October 1948. My first niece was so tiny that I looked at her and tactlessly remarked, "a Belsen baby." Moira took me to my first operas, *Aida* and *Madame Butterfly*. In *Aida* a diminutive Argentinian tenor comforted a huge Italian soprano, as they were imprisoned in a tomb and faced death together. Rina Malatrasi as Madame Butterfly swept me into a romantic world of a new intensity. Moira's two children brought fresh love and laughter into our family circle.

Jim was soon back in Melbourne, and received his FRACS (Fellow of the Royal Australian College of Surgeons). He became an honorary urological surgeon at Prince Henry's Hospital and the founding specialist in urology at the Repatriation Hospital. He also commenced private practice in his own rooms on Collins Street. Jim did the surgery, while Moira did the paperwork and looked after the running of the rooms as well as their family home. They were starting their careers and a family, and worked together as a wonderful team. They had eight children (five boys and three girls), all eventually university graduates: in medicine, law, veterinary science, economics, and engineering. Moira was the intellectual powerhouse behind their success, even if she jokingly referred to herself as the "family dropout," having never finished her own degree at the University of Melbourne. She considered her greatest achievement was the success of her children.

Settling Down

After buying their first home at 43 Lisson Grove, Hawthorn, where Justin and Joanna were born, they moved 234 Orrong Road, Toorak, where Bronwen, Mark, James, and Stephen were born. It was a spacious Spanish style house, with stucco exterior walls and tiles that possums delighted in upending. Always a rowdy household, it was full of fun and noise. Moira kept the children in check, as Jim worked extremely long hours. Their son Mark recalls how Moira "had a direct and beautiful way of putting things. When I was five or six, she sat me down and explained the family facts: her first obligation was 'to look after Dad and then you kids.' It was done in a loving way; it was just practical and the way it was. And Mum was a very practical woman."

At their home in Toorak, Moira and Jim entertained innumerable Australians and constantly welcomed international visitors—not only medical specialists but also others. In 1971 they gave a reception for a visiting Swiss professor and author, the enfant terrible of Catholic theology, Hans Küng. At another party in 1973 they entertained Jürgen Moltmann, a professor at the University of Tübingen and judged by many to be the leading Protestant theologian of his generation. That evening I could have brought to the gathering a Polish cardinal who was also visiting Melbourne, Karol Wojtyla. It became a little hard for Moira to forgive that oversight when five years later the cardinal became Pope John Paul II.

Every few years Moira and Jim recharged their relationship by spending several weeks abroad, attending international meetings of urologists and enjoying straight tourism. They shone as a charming and very good-looking couple. In Rio de Janeiro they met the President of Brazil and the legendary Russian astronaut, Yuri Gagarin. She joked with Gagarin about their both being small. No larger person could have fitted into the first manned space craft to orbit the earth. At a dinner in Rome, she sat next to Juan Fangio, the five time Formula One champion from Argentina. Moira did not speak Spanish and Fangio did not speak English. So they battled away in Italian. She asked: "What kind of car do you drive now?" "A Mercedes sedan," he replied, "and only at the speed limit." It was a wonderful evening, as she overcame the language barrier with her charm and infectious laugh.

Moira had few passions outside her husband and family. One was collecting antique furniture and old silver. Her mother (Joan) had an encyclopaedic knowledge of both and passed it on to her daughter. The two of them attended auction houses, where Moira made shrewd purchases for her home and then for her children. She had a very close relationship with Joan and, until Joan's death in 1977, talked with her virtually every day.

In 1961 Jim and Moira bought a property, Bunns Springs, north of Bordertown in South Australia. The whole family would work on the farm during school and university holidays. "It was the greatest education you could have," their son Mark told me. "Mum would drive to Bordertown for provisions and load the station wagon until it was bursting at the seams—to the bewilderment and delight of the shopkeepers who had nothing left on their shelves." He added: "she had boundless energy, cooking for twelve or fourteen people every day and running the household. It can only be said that she had two speeds, flat out and stop."

"Christmas days were the same," Mark continued. "Often she would cook ham and several turkeys for thirty people or more. It was a military exercise, with ten in the immediate family and countless cousins, aunts, and uncles. Dad would be presiding over the bar and Mum in the kitchen. The food was delicious. They were marvellous, happy times for all of us."

In the mid-sixties, Moira discovered skiing, and with other members of her family bought a flat at Falls Creek, in the Australian Alps. All her children spent the August school holidays skiing. Mark recalled how "we would be ejected from the flat at 8 a.m., and not allowed to return until 5 p.m. Sport was not one of her strong points. She broke her leg one year, received a plaster cast, and refused to go anywhere but back to the flat. Some friends came by next day and were horrified to find her mopping the floor on her hands and knees with her plaster cast wrapped in plastic." Mark finished by saying: "They were wonderful days skiing at Falls Creek and fishing there in the early summer. Skiing is still an important part of life for some of us, and we are so grateful to Mum for encouraging us to take it up."

Like her father, Moira had a deep dislike for injustice. At Bunns Springs she and Jim employed an indigenous worker named Ivan. She treasured Ivan and always gave him great encouragement—much to the annoyance of the manager's wife. She phoned Moira on a wintry, Sunday evening: "Tomorrow morning your Ivan will be brought before the magistrate on a charge of being drunk and disorderly." Up at five on Monday, Moira drove the five hours to Bordertown, arriving just in time to hear the testimony of a sergeant she knew.

Unfortunately for his case, the sergeant who arrested Ivan testified that his prisoner had been vomiting and lying in the gutter. As Ivan was unrepresented, Moira requested the magistrate's permission to speak on his behalf as an *amicus curiae* (friend of the court) and asked the sergeant: "Where did the accused spend the night?" "In the lockup, Mrs Peters." "Did you offer him a change of clothes after he was arrested?" "No, Mrs Peters." "Did you offer him laundry facilities?," she continued. "Of course not, we don't run a hotel here, Mrs Peters," the sergeant replied with evident sarcasm. At this point much laughter ran around the courtroom, until Moira delivered the *coup-de-grâce*. She turned to the magistrate and asked: "In view of the sergeant's testimony, can anyone explain how the accused is now wearing a clean shirt and looks so neat and tidy?" Silence. The magistrate looked at the sergeant and said: "Case dismissed."

Last Years

Eventually Moira and Jim sold the property at Bunns Springs and bought a smaller farm called Laurel Vale, right on top of the Dividing Range, an hour's drive north of Melbourne. They bred Angus cattle, and kept a bull called Murphy, and often had their grandchildren to stay. Early one morning a grandson rushed back into the house to announce: "Murphy's having breakfast with some kangaroos." Kangaroos had hopped across the fence and were grazing in the bull's paddock. But Murphy paid no notice to them as he chewed away on some hay.

Moira and Jim loved the rolling hills and beautiful views. It was their sanctuary. Every evening they sat on the front porch having a drink and chatting as the sun set over their western boundary.

They both drove a tractor and a land cruiser to drop bales of hay, slash ferns, or round up the cattle. Moira loved working in her vegetable and rose garden, while Jim was obsessed with slashing

Part II: Family

every stand of ferns on the property. Mark recalled the happy visits to Laurel Vale: "Mum would load us up with beautiful, fresh vegetables to take home after working on the farm. She never let us go home empty-handed. Many memorable family milestones were celebrated at Laurel Vale, including Sunday lunches, birthdays, and their fiftieth wedding anniversary, when all eight children gave rousing speeches."

After Jim died at home (in Toorak) in September 2010, Moira continued to run the farm until the Saturday on which she died. She and Jim had enjoyed close relations with local farmers and others. They continued to help her on the property right to the end. One of them was with Moira at Laurel Vale on the morning when she suffered a brain haemorrhage and fell unconscious. An ambulance picked her up, headed for Melbourne, and brought her to the closest, major hospital (in a suburb called Epping). A Vietnamese friend of mine, a Jesuit called Minh Tran, was the parish priest of Epping. He came instantly to the hospital and gave her the last rites. Sixteen of her children, their spouses, and grandchildren were gathered by her bedside when I pronounced a final blessing: "May the Lord bless you and keep you. May the Lord make his face shine upon you, and give you his peace." She died that Saturday evening shortly after eleven p.m.—proving until the last as little a burden to others as possible.

The funeral Mass took place in the chapel of Newman College, where Moira had been married over seventy years earlier. She had planned the order of service carefully, as she did everything, not wanting it to go beyond an hour. Hence only one person was to deliver a eulogy. A packed congregation heard her son Mark begin by saying: "With her striking red hair, Mum was vivacious, charming, and extraordinarily kind. She had a genuine interest in people, and won their admiration. She gave people respect, and they gave it back in spades. She was a pleasure to meet, and a pleasure to listen to."

Mark continued: "She never shirked hard work, and throughout her life organized all manner of events for family and friends. She was a practical woman, with a strong sense of justice, honesty, and high standards. She had a deep Catholic faith, and was devoted to her husband as he was to her." Calling her "the matriarch of our large and extended family," Mark added: "she always included everyone in important celebrations, the last being her ninetieth birthday. She had that happy knack of making everyone feel included and special."

Coming to the end of his eulogy, Mark said: "Mum set an example for all of us. She often remarked: 'Don't leave till tomorrow what you can do today.' It was a motto she lived by every day of her life. Mum was a doer, who ran not only a large household but also the finances for the farm, Dad's practice, and the family interests. Starting at 5.30 in the morning and finishing at 9.30 at night, she never stopped."

Mark paused and concluded: "She was a little dynamo, a great organizer and a wonderful encourager of all the people she knew. Her selfless devotion to her husband, children, brothers, and sisters was exemplary. We are here to celebrate a wonderful life well lived, all richer for having known her." Turning to the coffin, Mark ended: "We will all miss you, and we will all remember you with love and esteem, Little Mum."

Part II: Family

Moira and Me

Living overseas for many years, I kept in contact with Moira by letter, visits home to Melbourne, and meetings abroad. A very happy occasion came one Easter radiantly beautiful with flowers, when I flew from Rome to Washington, DC, and celebrated the wedding of her eldest daughter, Marion.

In the late seventies, Moira and Jim came to Rome in early June. Lecturing at the Gregorian University had just finished, an examination period (leisurely for the faculty) was starting, and the academic year was closing down. In June long days shine down on the eternal city, brilliant light fills the churches (you need it, as the ubiquitous baroque is short on windows), and the temperature has not yet risen to the sweltering heat of July and August.

Moira and Jim timed that visit to coincide with my birthday, June 2. Jim proposed an evening meal at the Domus Aurea, a grand restaurant built above Nero's palace (of the same name) on the Colle Oppio and overlooking the Colosseum. Since it was after all my birthday we were celebrating, Jim accepted my suggestion: the Vecchia Roma, a less expensive restaurant tucked away in a maze of narrow streets under the Capitol Hill and right on the edge of the old Jewish quarter. Jim's virtue was quickly rewarded.

We had scarcely been seated outside, under the sky of a pleasantly warm evening, when Anthony Quinn turned up with a party of six or seven. They took a table right behind me. Seated opposite me, Jim spent the meal discreetly observing the great actor who sat facing him across my shoulders. "Remarkably small hands for such a big man," Jim observed when we left the Vecchia Roma just before midnight. Quinn and his party were the only others still there as we walked off down a side street. We had gone only a few yards into the night, when we heard the sound of glasses being broken against a wall of the restaurant. Quinn and his party were repeating what he did in the film *Zorba the Greek*.

When the time approached for me to leave Rome, Moira worked behind the scenes with John Batt, an Anglican friend of ours who became a judge of the Court of Appeal of Victoria, to propose my name to the Australian government. They gathered a formidable group of "referees," including a retired Archbishop of Canterbury and two Americans. In January 2006 I was created a Companion of the General Division of the Order of Australia (AC), the highest civil honour granted through the Australian government. Some months earlier, an official in Canberra contacted me confidentially to ask whether I would accept the honour. At once I wrote a letter of acceptance, thinking, "This will please Moira." At the time I knew nothing of how much she had been involved in promoting my cause.

When I returned to live permanently in Australia, Moira generously organized a welcome home for me and then, two years later on June 2, 2011, a reception for my eightieth birthday held at the Melbourne Club. For many years she had seized such occasions to celebrate milestones in my life; the first was an at home when I was ordained a priest in January 1963.

Back in Australia, I began publishing my memoirs: *A Midlife Journey* (2012), *The Left Bank of the Tiber* (2013), and *From Rome to Royal Park* (2015). Moira revelled in the launches of the trilogy. Tim Fischer, a former Deputy Prime Minister of Australia and Ambassador of Australia to the Holy See (2009–2012), launched *A Midlife Journey* at Xavier College, his and my old high school. Since his home was far away in Southern New South Wales, he had been a boarder at the school, and had stayed weekends at Moira's home with her eldest son, Stewart, a fellow schoolboy at Xavier. Tim also launched *The Left Bank of the Tiber*. From that evening I have kept a cheerful photograph of Tim and myself flanking Moira, elegantly dressed and smiling happily.

The epitome of tireless hospitality Moira shone at such social and family occasions. Right to the end, she remained closely interested in the doings of her family and many friends. The happy years of childhood at Rock Lodge gave her an unstoppable joy in life and great practical wisdom. I could not have wished for a better eldest sister. I had bonded closely with her from my earliest years, and found her the best of friends.

Appendix: Homily preached at her funeral, October 20, 2017, in the chapel of Newman College.

"*Blessed are the merciful, blessed are the peace-makers.*"

Since Moira Peters died last Saturday night, messages have poured in from relatives and friends. One person e-mailed me: "She was a wonderful woman and will be mightily missed." Another person said: "Moira was a dear friend to my wife and me. She lived a fulfilling life to the end." Someone else, who has suffered a great deal in life, wrote: "Moira has been steadfast in her love and mercy. A genuine peacemaker, exemplar, and rock of virtue." Yet another person remarked: "Moira was so energetic, engaging, and clearly delighting in life." Another put it this way: "She was such a lovely person, so kind, so thoughtful, so aware of other people's needs." Others contented themselves with saying, "Moira was always so kind to me." Or, "Moira was a truly incredible person. She was a delight."

What was Moira's secret? What was the secret at the heart of her existence? What made this courageous, valiant woman so special? I think it was her being a person **for others**. Simply by being born into this world, we are all persons **with other people**. For years, perhaps even all our life long, we face the struggle of moving from being **merely with other people** to living **for other people**. But Moira, from the start, lived for other people.

We might sum up what Jesus said in the beatitudes that way. Be merciful, be a peace-maker. Be all those other things which will make you a person who lives **for other people.**

Right through life, Moira always offered other people her unfailing support and encouragement. She gave her husband, her children, her wider family, her friends, and many, many other people her constant interest and love. Right to the end she remained intensely involved in all the doings of her children, grandchildren and great-granddaughters. She was generous to all, and untiringly supportive of all.

Moira had a formidable intellect and many talents. She was dux of her school. In what we now call the Year 12 exams, she achieved first-class honours in English, History, Italian and Japanese. She was third in the state in English, and won the exhibition in Japanese. She could easily have been a first-rate barrister, a university professor, or a federal parliamentarian. But she found her deep fulfilment in living for others, encouraging them, and rejoicing in all their various achievements.

For many years I lived overseas, a long way from Moira. But she was always there with me. When some difficult decision came up or some problematic situation confronted me, I would ask myself: Now what advice would Moisie offer me? What would **she** do in this situation? Invariably it was good advice, and I never regretted asking myself: What advice would Moisie give me?

Jesus called himself the bread of life. He is **the** bread of life who feeds a deeply fulfilled life here and now, as well as in the life to come. Jesus **is** the bread of life, both here and hereafter. If I dare speak for him, I think Jesus must have delighted in the hospitality that Moira unwaveringly offered to so many people. Jesus was and is a uniquely hospitable person. He welcomed and welcomes everyone into his presence and to his table. Moira did just that, welcoming everyone into her presence and to her table. In her own way, she was the bread of life for others. Because she did that, she lived a truly happy and fulfilling life to the very end. She was a tireless blessing to others, and the good Lord blessed her in turn.

So many of Moira's family were residents at Newman College; she was married in this Chapel of the Holy Spirit in 1946. Now she is being buried from this same chapel on 20 October, the birthday of her beloved husband, Jim.

At the end, the good Lord saw to it that Moira died quickly and easily-- only a few hours after suffering a massive stroke. The good Lord saw to it also that she died surrounded by sixteen members of her family, including eight of her grandchildren.

Now Moisie is with her beloved husband Jim, with her parents Joan and Frank, with her siblings Dympna, Jim, and Glynn, and with so many relatives, friends, and others whom she loved and cared for unfailingly in this life.

Moisie, thank you **so much** for everything. Moisie, you did us all proud. Moisie, pray for us all.

8
James ("Jim") Patrick O'Collins (1932-2017)

Eighteen months younger than me, my brother Jim would become one of the busiest urologists of his generation and contribute to the remarkable progress in treating the urinary system made during his years in that specialized field of surgery. Glynn (b. 1934) came next, the last surviving child of my parents. We all loved Glynn spontaneously. A freckled, affectionate redhead, he was often sickly, but grew up to be a fine athlete and champion golfer. He was to follow Jim in studying medicine, but, unlike Jim, took up radiology. Although the youngest of the six children, sadly Glynn was the first one of us six children to die—of cancer, in 2003.

Jim, Glynn, and myself began our schooling at home, joining our three older sisters in being taught reading, writing, and arithmetic by a strict governess, Miss Gilder. After World War II broke out, like myself, Jim and Glynn took an intense interest in recognizing military aircraft and tanks, both "ours" and "theirs." They joined me in "digging for victory," though not by growing vegetables. I inspected plans for air-raid shelters and decided to build one for our family, at the top of a back drive to our property and close to the house, Rock Lodge. We gave up after digging a trench over three feet deep in the clay. Later some soil was dumped into the trench and a row of agapanthus planted there.

In early 1942, the three of us began at St Francis Xavier's, a Catholic primary school about three miles away. I was aged ten, Jim nine, and Glynn not quite eight. We rode horses to school or went on bicycles. In what was our initiation into regular schooling and our first prolonged contact with other boys and girls, we supported each other well. Together we grew to hate the jam sandwiches or peanut-butter sandwiches Mother prepared for our lunch.

Our transition from home to school went remarkably smoothly. We had seen many of the hundred or so pupils at Sunday Mass, where some of them occupied the front pews. The place itself was familiar to us, as the teaching took place right in the church—the ultimate in identification between Catholicism and education. During the week, sliding screens cut off the sanctuary and formed two large class rooms out of the nave. A glass enclosed veranda added two further class rooms for the top grades. Boys and girls could continue at the school until they finished the eighth grade around the age of thirteen. Some sat for the merit certificate, a state examination. A few went on to high school. There were no fees, but the children brought a shilling or so each week from their parents.

Jim and Glynn were with me again as boarders at Xavier College, Kew (Melbourne). In February 1944 I began five years there; Jim arrived in 1945 and Glynn in 1947. Jim was already a voracious reader and did well at studies, soon showing his aptitude for things scientific. As the science teacher, Fr "Butter" McCarthy, failed to teach them much, Jim and a friend, Henry Burger, sat at the back and studied physics and chemistry for themselves.[25] When mathematical questions emerged, they consulted Ian Howells, a brilliant mathematician in a higher class who was later elected a fellow at Trinity College, Cambridge, before entering the Jesuit Order. Inevitably the systematic inattention on the part of Jim and Henry proved too much for "Butter." He packed them off to receive the strap from the Prefect of Studies, Fr John Rolland ("Caesar") Boylen. Thoroughly abreast of the situation, Caesar asked: "Milk and sugar?" He served the two boys morning tea, chatted for a while, and sent them back to class with the request: "Please look suitably chastened."

At Xavier College itself, Jim, Glynn and I rarely had the chance of being together much. But we sometimes went into the city to see a film or lunch with our parents. Father ran the King's Theatre, which occasionally staged live shows like *The Desert Song* (an operetta with lyrics by Oscar Hammerstein), but mostly offered films. We went back repeatedly to see a long-running success, *Casablanca* starring Humphrey Bogart, Ingrid Bergman, Paul Henreid, and Claude Rains. Through the manager of the King's, we could get free tickets to a number of other city cinemas. Later, during their medical studies at the University of Melbourne, Glynn and Jim sometimes put on dinner jackets and worked in the evenings as managers for one of Father's four cinemas.

In our years at Xavier, Jim, Glynn, and I sometime spent holidays with our uncle, James Patrick O'Collins, the bishop of Ballarat. He was Jim's godfather and close friend. He lived in a massive, bluestone house at Ballarat, a former gold-mining town about seventy miles from Melbourne. A short, thick-set man with dark

---

[25] During his medical course at the University of Melbourne, Burger won eleven of the twelve prizes on offer. He became a world class endocrinologist.

hair, uncle Jim enjoyed excellent health, worked hard, and always seemed imperturbable. He summed up his philosophy of life by saying: "Keep your nose dry, your mouth shut, and your bowels open." In a part of Australia where it can snow during the winter, he slept on a veranda, exposed to winds and night frosts. He and Father were extraordinarily fond of each other, and that made us three boys instantly at home with him.

We enjoyed the run of the bishop's mansion—in those days it was called the bishop's "palace"— with its high ceilings, nineteenth-century bathrooms, brass-knobbed beds, tiled floors, and bounteous food. For some years we called him "my Lord," and eventually "Uncle Jim." His grand-nephews and -nieces were to refer to him as "Uncle J the B." He had inherited from his predecessor a fine cook, who felt it her duty to fatten his nephews, nieces, and any other relatives who came to stay. The bishop's property, although surrounded by suburban housing, was large enough to provide grazing for several cows. Gradually Uncle Jim replaced a potato field with lawns, put in fish ponds, and built aviaries. Lake Wendouree, on which rowing events for the 1956 Olympic Games were held, lay a few yards beyond the back fence. Around the shores stretched botanical gardens, where we chased squirrels and tried our luck in getting into and out of a maze. We took rides on the quaint Ballarat trams, went to cinemas, and visited the Eureka Stockade, the scene in 1854 of Australia's only "revolution," a brief and bloody stand by gold miners against oppressive taxes.

At home on our parents' property down Port Phillip Bay from Melbourne, Jim, Glynn, and I played cricket, football, golf, and tennis together. On one occasion Jim covered himself with nets to lead us on a wild attempt to rob a native beehive. We failed when the ladder that Glynn and I were holding for him broke. On the beach one day we came across two fisherman who had netted a large school of salmon. They invited us to wade into the shallow water and help ourselves. Glynn and I grabbed a couple of fish, but Jim systematically hunted down the largest salmon in the catch.

During the middle and late 1940s, relatives and friends often came to stay at Rock Lodge. A cottage at the entrance to the property provided extra bedrooms; for a time we also had the use of a large caravan parked down the back drive. When Uncle Jim came, he brought with him a battered suitcase containing the vestments, vessels, and missal needed to celebrate the Eucharist for us at home. Jim, Glynn, and I had to remember an extra washing of the hands and the variations in the Latin responses required when serving Mass for a bishop.

During the long and lovely summer of 1945/46, we prepared for the first break in the family circle, Moira's wedding to Jim Peters. A dark-haired, stunningly handsome man, he had been a champion footballer for the Melbourne Blacks in the 1930s. Twelve years older than Moira, he was close to my Father, who advised him on business matters, played golf with him, and constantly enjoyed his company. When he stayed at Rock Lodge, Jim Peters slept in one of the bunks in the two bedrooms shared by my brothers and myself. Once when he and Moira were out for an evening, we sewed up the legs of his pyjamas, and kept awake to hear him quietly swear away to himself as he undressed in the dark and discovered what had happened.

By the time he had finished his high school studies at Xavier College at the end of 1949, my brother Jim had decided on a medical career. But first he took a gap year driving around Europe with our sister Maev and a cousin Deirdre Lewis. Later he never failed to "get a rise" out of Maev by describing their visit to Lourdes, the shrine of the Blessed Virgin Mary in the south of France. According to Jim, the day ended with the two girls drinking too much; he had to carry them up to their room.

In early 1951, Jim became a student at Newman College, and in 1957 would graduate MB BS (bachelor of medicine, bachelor of surgery) at the University of Melbourne. Father had been resident at Newman for four years, was a close friend of Father Jeremiah Murphy (the rector), and belonged to the College Council until his death in 1961.

This made Newman a home away from home for Jim, and he hit the ground running. Instructed by senior students at initiation to do something special, he and others (including a graduate student from Trinity who suggested the raid) took a pickup truck around to Trinity College and started loading a few statues from the grounds. When the warden happened to pass by, Jim assured him: "as old-Trinity boys we're ashamed of the state of the statues. We're taking them away to clean them up." In fact, without damaging them, Jim and his mates lined the statues up around the grave of a Trinity old-boy in Melbourne General Cemetery, and then sent a note to tell the college where to find them.

With the robust frame of a good boxer, Jim enjoyed intercollegiate sport, leading the Newman College teams in golf, athletics, and (the seconds in) football. After two years the golf team began winning; it now included his younger brother Glynn, the golf champion of Australian Universities. After disastrously low results in intercollegiate athletics, Father Murphy encouraged Jim to take things in hand. Jim badgered other students into cutting back on smoking and doing some serious training; the Newman team was pipped at the post in the very last race. Jim was rolling a keg of beer to the party when he ran into Father Murphy, who remarked: "Lourdes water, I suppose. Have a good evening." In those days Ormond College had one or two students who, because they played VFL (Victorian Football League) football, were not permitted to play on their first team for their college. Jim revelled in irritating Ken Melville, a theological student of Ormond, who played center for Melbourne in the VFL but could be annoyed into giving away free kicks in games against the very amateur players of Newman College seconds. The prank Jim treasured all his life involved gate-crashing a function in St Kilda by arriving in a former hearse, a 1927 Stanley Steamer[26] with all on board dressed as undertakers in black cloaks and top hats. Once inside the gate, they solemnly carried into the building a coffin full of grog. In those days strict liquor laws could make it difficult to bring beer, wine, and spirits to social functions.

Jim sailed through his medical studies, helped by Harry and Gerry Crock, identical twins two years ahead of him in the College who shone as students and later (Harry as an orthopaedic surgeon and Gerry as a professor of opthalmology). But Professor (later Sir) Roy Douglas ("Pansy") Wright decided to teach Jim a lesson for not turning up to do his laboratory work. Failing in physiology, Jim had to re-take the examination three months later. He had not known that the young lady who checked attendance in the lab was Wright's niece. But there was no ill will involved. When Jim and other medical students cooked a barbecue at the back of Jimmy Watson's wine bar in nearby Lygon Street, Pansy bought them the wine.

After graduation Jim spent a year of residency at the Mater

---

[26] The twins Francis and Freelan Stanley created a vehicle, run on the steam generated by a boiler and commonly called "The Stanley Steamer," which sold well initially but ceased production in the 1920s.

Hospital, Brisbane, working as a casualty surgeon and urologist. When he returned to St Vincent's Hospital, Melbourne (for a year as Pathology Registrar and then Senior Registrar in Surgery), he lived in Newman College, gave tutorials, and once again enjoyed Fr Murphy's company (who "served better port than wine"). Jim topped the course for the first part of his FRACS (Fellow of the Royal Australasian College of Surgeons) before leaving for London and a course at St Thomas' Hospital. Having already completed the first part of his FRACS, in England he could take the second part of his FRCS (Fellow of the Royal College of Surgeons) in March 1961 and again topped his group.

Three years of enriching practice in England began with an appointment as Senior Registrar in Orthopaedics at St Mary's Hospital, Paddington. Jim then moved north to work in Leeds as a urologist at St James' University Hospital (popularly known as "Jimmy's"). He came to know Jack Shaw, a dealer in antique silver, who lived in a village on the nearby Yorkshire moors. Jim was happy to steal a march on Mother by identifying and buying old silver from a remote but fascinating dealer. At the end of 1962 he was appointed Senior Registrar at the Bradford Royal Infirmary. A year later he left for the United States and became a visiting fellow in New York, Boston, Cleveland, Rochester (Minnesota), San Francisco and Los Angeles, at hospitals and centers which included the Massachusetts General Hospital, the Cleveland Clinic, and the Mayo Clinic.

Returning to Melbourne and taking up an appointment as a research fellow at the Children's Hospital, in 1964 Jim topped the second part of his FRACS (in urology). From December 1965 to May 1966, he served in Vietnam, where he ran a hospital close to the Cambodian border. Attached to the South Vietnam army as a colonel, he was the only urologist in Vietnam. But his main concern was with other areas of medicine—in particular, the high incidence of tuberculosis and similar diseases. He succeeded in lowering the mortality rate at his hospital from 33% to 9%.

Back in Melbourne, Jim became assistant urologist at Prince Henry's Hospital. But, persuaded by the growth of population to the South-East of the city, he started urological units at Dandenong District Hospital and Frankston Hospital. He also operated regularly down the Mornington Peninsula, as well as at centers to the East in Gippsland. During the 1977 federal elections, his prize patient at Frankston Hospital was the local member who was also the Deputy Leader of the Liberal Party, Phillip Lynch. Jim received anxious phone calls from the Prime Minister, Malcolm Fraser, and kept assuring him, "Don't worry, Malcolm. I'm keeping him in hospital and making sure the press can't get to him." At the time Lynch was under fire over an alleged conflict of interests involving a family trust, but was subsequently cleared by an official inquiry that followed the elections.

Head of surgery at Frankston Hospital for many years, from 1970 to 1990 Jim was the busiest and, arguably, the top urologist in all Australia, and had many stories to tell. One patient, an ex-policeman turned contract killer, was so grateful for being fixed up that he told Jim: "Doctor, I owe you one. If you have a problem and can't go to the police, here's my phone number."

Married in 1967 by his godfather (Bishop O'Collins) to Rosemary ("Posey") Calder in the chapel of Newman College, Jim treasured his work in Frankston and life with his wife and two children (who both became Newman students) at the family home. He declined tempting appointments from elsewhere.

One Italian surgeon, who headed the best Italian urological unit (in Padua), invited Jim in 1972 to take up a permanent position, but on the condition that he would spend two weeks each month working in the Soviet Union. This Italian had been operating there and treated, among others, the Russian leader Yuri Andropov, whose condition, however, deteriorated. When Jim visited Padua in 1978, the Italian urologist looked worried; he died a year later of a "heart attack." Jim often wondered out loud about the true cause of his death. Kept alive on dialysis by Algerian urologists, Andropov himself passed away in February 1984.

Another Italian surgeon, who operated on members of the Mafia, invited Jim to join him in Florence. Jim declined the offer, but met the Mafia in a different setting. Shortly after the judge Giovanni Falcone and the prosecutor Paolo Borsellino, along with their police escorts, were assassinated in 1990, Jim and Posey headed to a hotel in Cefalu for a Sicilian holiday. On arrival they discovered that the Mafia owned the hotel and had gathered there for a wedding. Suddenly the whole area was surrounded by up to a thousand "Alpini," crack Italian soldiers sent to Sicily in an Anti-Mafia war. The stand-off between the Mafia and the Alpini was complicated by neighbours of the hotel, wealthy oil chiefs from the Middle East. The Mafia in the hotel suspected Jim of being a member of the FBI, but their "capo" decided against any drastic action. After Jim and Posey were allowed to leave, this time it was Posey's turn. When passing through a checkpoint of the Alpini, she had a gun pointed at her head.

An outstanding surgeon, Jim prized the anaesthetists, radiologists, theatre sisters, and others who worked with him. But he grumbled about the bureaucrats, whom he believed often wasted funds without producing better health care for the wider public. An unfailingly courageous person, for the last fifteen years of his life, Jim struggled with cancer—eventually, three forms of cancer. His wife Posey cared for him with unfailing love.

Over the years I received unbounded kindness from Jim, Posey, and their children. When I was about to leave Australia in 1973 for what turned out to be thirty-six years overseas (in the UK and Italy), they farewelled me at an elegant dinner party for my closest friends in Rock Lodge, our home which they had inherited and recently renovated. The great mahogany table, around which the dining room had been built, gleamed with antique silver, and family portraits looked down on us from the walls. Years later I could share with them a similar dinner—at high table in Pembroke College, University of Cambridge, when they came to England in 1991 for the wedding of Posey's niece. They stayed in the Catholic chaplaincy to the University, Fisher House, a marvellous, sixteenth-century, timbered building with low, wooden ceilings. They slept in the same bed that Cardinal Joseph Ratzinger occupied when he visited three years earlier. After his election to the papacy in 2005, that upstairs room came to be called "the papal chamber."

During my years in Rome (1974–2006), Jim turned up regularly in Rome with Posey and their two children, James ("Jamie") and Victoria ("Tori"). One cold but clear Christmas morning when the scent of roasted chestnuts drifted down the streets, Tori went with her parents and Jamie to receive her first Communion from Pope John Paul II at a Mass in St Peter's Basilica. During those visits I put them in contact with my local friends, not least Frank and Orietta Pogson Doria Pamphilj. Memory supplies the picture of Orietta showing the two children the secrets of the Palazzo Doria. They included a sliding door behind which Orietta and her parents had hidden when German soldiers raided their home in late 1943. The tall, Italian princess strode down the corridors initiating the delighted, Australian children into some of the mysteries of a gigantic Roman palace.

In the early summer of 1989, Jim and Posey arrived for a medical conference sponsored by the Pontifical Council of Health Care. I was startled when he told me the theme of the conference: male impotence. He too had been surprised (and pleased) to find the Vatican inviting specialists like himself to share information about ways of dealing with impotence caused by operations on the prostate (about 60% of the cases of impotence).

Then Jim learned from the Pontifical Council that the idea of the conference came from John Paul II himself. Knowing how marriages can be threatened and even wrecked when surgery makes a husband incapable of normal sexual relations, the Pope had brought together experts to discuss means for restoring such relations. John Paul II's loving concern for married people went beyond describing matters "from first principles," as he often did, to encourage practical solutions based on evidence and experience. Jim was satisfied that the conference of specialists brought some progress in dealing with male impotence.

Jim and Posey came to Rome for a celebration of my seventieth birthday, June 2, 2001: a formal presentation of a book written in my honour,[27] followed by a reception at the Gregorian University, a dinner that evening (which Jim generously paid for), and lunch the next day in the garden of the British Embassy to the Holy See. For the occasion, George and Eileen Carey flew down to Rome. Still Archbishop of Canterbury, George wrote the foreword for the *Festschrift*.

---

[27] Daniel Kendall and Stephen T. Davis (eds), *The Convergence of Theology* (Mahwah, NJ: Paulist Press, 2001).

Part II: Family

There was instant rapport between Jim and the Archbishop, who invited him and Posey to stay with him and Eileen in London or Canterbury. Sadly it was an invitation that could not be taken up. The following year Jim began his pilgrimages to clinics: to Cabrini Hospital, to Cabrini Rehabilitation, and, finally, to Cabrini Palliative Care. Let me append the homily I preached at the funeral Mass for Jim in the chapel of Newman College, on March 9, 2017.

*****

"Some of you present this afternoon will have enjoyed years ago the musical about Jesus Christ, *Godspell*. One or two of you may have played in *Godspell* when your school put on that musical. Three of the memorable lines from *Godspell* formed a prayer sung to Christ: 'to know thee more clearly, love thee more dearly, and follow thee more nearly.' Those lines were taken from a hauntingly beautiful prayer by the medieval Christian bishop, St Richard of Chichester. You find the prayer in front of his tomb in Chichester, down on the coast in the south of England. The whole prayer runs like this: 'Thanks be to thee, my Lord Jesus Christ, for all the benefits which thou hast given me, for all the pains and insults thou hast borne for me. O most merciful Redeemer, Friend, and Brother, may I know thee more clearly, love thee more dearly and follow thee more nearly.'

St Richard of Chichester addressed Christ as being both his friend and his brother, a brother who was also a uniquely dear friend. In the last few years, that line from St Richard has come to me repeatedly when I thought about my own brother Jim. Jim was a brother who was also a very dear friend; he was both friend and brother, a brother whom God and my parents gave to me, a brother who was always a treasured friend.

Jim was blessed with remarkable gifts. He used his gifts with first rate skill and courageous tenacity as an outstanding surgeon. Recently when he lay dying in Cabrini Palliative Care Hospice, I held his hands and thought how his surgeon's hands had brought healing and health to thousands of people. Those hands saved innumerable lives, and gave people years of comfortable living. I always admired my brother for the generous, committed, and expert way he used his great gifts in the service of others. The hands of a surgeon symbolize so much effective love, a love well practised.

But friendship and love are much more than mere admiration. Over the years, Jim occasionally talked with me about love. Only a few weeks ago, as life was slipping away from him, he raised with me the question: 'What is perfect love?' It's a great question: what is perfect love? The question leads us to a further question: Who is perfect love? In whose life do we find perfect love?

Last year Pope Francis published *The Joy of Love*, a remarkable exhortation on love: married love and family love. It's a document that speaks the language of everyday life, a document that knows how important it is for married and family love to say frequently: please, thank you, and sorry. Those three expressions are vital, if married and family love is to survive and flourish: please, thank you, and sorry.

In his exhortation *The Joy of Love*, Pope Francis did something no pope had ever done before him by quoting novelists, poets and an outstanding Danish film, *Babette's Feast*. The Pope knows that novels, poetry and great films have wonderful things to say about love, our love for one another and our love for God. So too do some pieces of music, both operatic arias and popular songs. After the American composer Irving Berlin wrote his lyric, 'I'll be loving you always,' he played it for a friend. The friend then asked him:

Part II: Family

'Why don't you call your song 'I'll be loving you Thursday'?' 'After all,' the friend continued, 'Love breaks down; relationships come to an end; diamonds may not be forever.' But Irving Berlin refused to change his words and published a very successful song, 'I'll be loving you always.' As far as Irving Berlin was concerned, diamonds are forever. He dedicated his new song to his wife, to whom he had been happily married for many years.

I never quoted Irving Berlin to my brother Jim. I should have, as Jim clearly shared Berlin's sentiments. For Jim, Posey was the heart of his existence. They were married for 49 years, and would have celebrated their golden anniversary next month, on April 28.

Our love goes out to people, but it also goes out to institutions, like Newman College. Jim loved this college: he studied here for six years before graduating MB BS at the University of Melbourne. Then he came back to Newman for a couple of years of residence when he became Pathology Registrar and then Senior Registrar in Surgery at St Vincent's Hospital. In 1967, Jim was married in this chapel, and now he has returned for his final farewell in the same chapel.

Love for people and love for places binds our life together. We spend our lives, supported by love, challenged by love and struggling with the realities of love. I found it so right that as he lay dying, Jim would ask himself: 'What is perfect love?' Yes, and who is perfect love, and who is love in person? St Richard of Chichester pointed us in the right direction when he prayed: 'Thanks be to thee, my Lord Jesus Christ, for all the benefits which thou hast given me, for all the pains and insults which thou hast borne for me. O most merciful Redeemer, Friend and Brother, may I know thee more clearly, love thee more dearly, and follow thee more nearly.'

Part III: Friends

9
Mother (St) Teresa of Calcutta (1910–1997)

This third part was envisaged as presenting portraits in alphabetical order. But it seems rather odd to enforce that rule, since it would mean starting from Geoffrey Chapman and arriving in last place at a canonized saint Teresa of Calcutta. In any case every good rule deserves to be broken once.

India, Australia, and the United States

In 1978, I wrote about Mother Teresa as a contemporary example of a midlife journey, triggered in her case by a desire for "something more."[28] At the age of nineteen she travelled out to India and began work in the Bengal Mission of the Loreto Sisters. Completing her first journey meant physically moving away from her happy home in Yugoslavia to a new place on the far side of the

---

[28] G. O'Collins, *The Second Journey: Spiritual Awareness and the Mid-Life Crisis* (New York: Paulist Press, 1978).

world. She went through the stages others expected of her, taking her first vows in 1931 and then her final vows in 1937. She had settled down in what looked like a permanent role.

But nine years later she felt "a call within a call." "It was," she reflected, "a vocation to give up even Loreto where I was very happy and to go out in the streets to serve the poorest of the poor." Significantly, this experience took place on a journey—from Calcutta to the Himalayas. She recalled the day: "In 1946 I was going to Darjeeling to make my retreat. It was in that train, I heard the call to give up all and follow him [God] into the slums to serve him among the poorest of the poor."

She applied for the necessary permissions to leave the convent and strike out on her own. Two years later all the official approvals had come through. Mother Teresa left the beautiful garden and "the quiet, peaceful place" that had been her religious home. She walked out alone onto the streets of Calcutta. Soon, however, she had established a new and enduring community of sisters whose work for the dying, the utterly poor, and the incurably ill came to inspire people around the world to share this kind of love in action.[29]

We should have little difficulty in spotting some typical features of a midlife journey. An inner voice on a long train ride led a nun in her mid-thirties to discover the program for the second half of her life. This second journey let her work with tremendous energy to relieve human misery and do, as she repeatedly put it, "something beautiful for God."

In *The Second Journey* I put Mother Teresa alongside other

---

[29] The quotations are taken from Malcolm Muggeridge, *Something Beautiful for God: Mother Teresa of Calcutta* (London: Collins, 1971).

notable Christians, like St Ignatius Loyola, John Wesley, Blessed John Henry Newman, and Dietrich Bonhoeffer. In their middle years, they left earlier dreams behind and accepted a new and fruitful course in their lives.

On a short visit to Calcutta in February 1971, I came close to meeting Mother Teresa. Ian Travers-Ball, who had been a fellow novice in Australia twenty years earlier took me to see his ministry among the derelict, the dying, and the terribly poor. As an ordained priest he had ceased to be a Jesuit, so that as Brother Andrew he could create a congregation of men to work alongside Mother Teresa's nuns. Both she and Ian had followed a call that took them away from their settled place in the world to accept the risks involved in new enterprises. About two dozen people lived in the small house that served as Ian's headquarters. I came away from there boosted by the gentle happiness with which they shared all things and thinking to myself: "This is what the early Christians were like."

The following year I became part of a committee that helped to plan an ecumenical conference that would be part of the Fortieth International Eucharistic Conference that took place in Melbourne (February 18–25, 1973). Archbishop James Knox left us free to invite anyone we wished, provided we invited Mother Teresa and paid our bills. Before he was appointed to lead the Catholic Archdiocese of Melbourne, he had lived in India as apostolic nuncio, met her, and came to esteem her highly. She accepted our invitation and the highlight of her presence was sharing the platform in the Melbourne Town Hall with Jürgen Moltmann, a world-ranking Protestant theologian, famous for his best-selling book on hope. That evening three thousand people heard him speak on the theology of peace and Mother Teresa speak on the Christian vocation to spread peace. Moltmann teased me afterwards: "Is that what you wanted to do at the Eucharistic Congress? Make a team out of a Catholic saint and a leading Protestant theologian?" "Jürgen," I replied, "that recipe will never let you down."

When Mother Teresa received the Nobel Peace Prize in 1979, I felt that our ecumenical committee in Melbourne had stolen a march on the judges for that prize. Six years earlier we presented her to a national and international audience as a power for world peace.

During the 1973 congress, a visiting Polish cardinal, Karol Wojtyla, first met Mother Teresa. Their friendship flourished, in life and in death. He lived long enough as Pope John Paul II to declare her a "blessed" in 2003, a stage before she became a canonized saint under Pope Francis on September 4, 2016. Eventually I was to insert among the illustrations of both *Catholicism* and *Catholicism: A Very Short Introduction* photographs of John Paul II embracing Mother Teresa.[30] The 1973 congress also gave me a chance of meeting her and continuing to meet her, after she established a community in Melbourne.

I sometimes celebrated the Eucharist for her sisters in a battered, inner-city dwelling where they gave shelter and food to the homeless. One morning I had put on the vestments and was about to say Mass at 7 a.m., when in came Mother Teresa and a pretty, mini-skirted young woman. "You will preach on religious life, won't you Father," she said to me. I had only five minutes to think up something useful to say. After Mass the young lady returned, now dressed in the white and blue colours of the Missionaries of

---

[30] G. O'Collins and M. Farrugia, *Catholicism: The Story of Catholic Christianity*, 2nd edn (Oxford: Oxford University Press, 2015), 376; G. O'Collins, *Catholicism: A Very Short Introduction*, 2nd edn (Oxford: Oxford University Press, 2017), 109.

Charity and carrying the skirt, blouse, and other clothing she had been wearing an hour before and which she now deposited in the arms of some relative or friend.

As well as being marvellously mystical, Mother Teresa could be practical and peremptory. On one visit to Melbourne she hailed a taxi and asked the driver: "How long does it take to get to Broken Hill?" (She was thinking of opening a house in that mining city in the south-west of New South Wales.) "The best part of a day," the driver told her. "Well, we better start right now," she told the startled man as she and another sister stepped into the taxi.

In 1976 I was invited to speak at the Eucharistic Congress in Philadelphia, held on the occasion of two hundred years since the American Declaration of Independence. On the plane out of Rome I had the good fortune to sit next to Mother Teresa, who was also en route to Philadelphia. We chatted about various things, including the good effect she had on Malcolm Muggeridge. His latest book confirmed the fact that he had come to full faith in Christ. In Philadelphia I found myself in the same hotel as Mother Teresa. The other guests included Archbishop Helder Camara from Brazil, the American theologian Avery (later Cardinal) Dulles, Prince Rainier and Princess Grace of Monaco, and other speakers. A bellhop asked me: "Where's *that* nun? I want to shake hands with her before they canonize her." I went looking for her and brought her to the bellhop. Mother Teresa smiled at him, shook his hand, and wrote on a piece of paper: "Let us love one another as Jesus has loved us."

The hotel had just been the headquarters for a July meeting of the American Legion, a very large association made up of veterans of World War I, World War II, the Korean War, and the

Vietnam War. Twenty-six people, almost all Legionnaires, caught a mysterious new disease and died. News was beginning to come through about the deaths and the connection with the Bellevue Stratford, the hotel where we were staying for the Eucharistic Congress. Afterwards I mused: "If the disease had continued to strike during the Eucharistic Congress, I might have slipped into heaven behind Mother Teresa and the former Grace Kelly, now Princess Grace of Monaco."

When Mother Teresa finished her major speech at the congress, Helder Camara, the saintly Brazilian campaigner for the hungry and the oppressed, who always looked to me like a cheerful leprechaun, sprang to his feet and embraced her. The straitlaced Archbishop Giovanni Benelli, soon to leave the Vatican and become the (Cardinal) Archbishop of Florence, was the third figure on the platform. He looked startled, but, in front of an audience of several thousand people, had no choice. He had to get up himself and embrace Mother Teresa and Helder Camara.

A Saint and an Individual

It was always compellingly clear what Mother Teresa wanted, no matter whom she was engaged with. In Rome she called on Cardinal Agostino Casaroli, John Paul II's admirable Secretary of State (1979–90), and asked for a place right in Vatican City where her sisters could live and care for the homeless. "That's a beautiful idea," Casaroli said, "but we don't have suitable building to make available for the project." He was deluded into thinking that she would take "no" for an answer. Mother Teresa left his office and took a seat in his waiting room—"doing a squat," as Indians say. Naturally she caught the attention of all the bishops and other officials coming to see the cardinal. "Mother Teresa is sitting outside," they kept telling him. After an hour or so, the pressure proved too much. A frustrated Cardinal Casaroli burst into the waiting room and told her: "Yes, we'll find you a place."

The shelter sits right on the edge of the Piazza del Santo Ufficio, a stone's throw from the *palazzo* housing what is now called the Congregation for the Doctrine of the Faith, rather than the Holy Office of the Inquisition. The scene is humanized by the sisters of Mother Teresa and the homeless. I still puzzle over Cardinal Casaroli's initial refusal. On weekends he regularly visited a gaol for juvenile offenders, and as "Padre Agostino" generously supported and encouraged the young men.

The Casaroli exchange typified what it meant to be Mother Teresa. Some years later on a lecturing visit to San Diego, California, I learned that she had just been hospitalized there and brought back to life by a team of expert doctors. When she started recovering, she wanted to have the team come to her hospital room for the celebration of Mass. At once one of the doctors rushed off to the local Catholic bishop and told him about Mother Teresa's invitation, adding: "The problem is that I'm Jewish. What should I do?" Without hesitation the bishop replied: "Do what we all do. Do what she tells you."

A day or so later the same bishop celebrated Mass in Mother Teresa's room. At the end she prayed silently for some minutes, and then fished out from under the sheets a contract prepared for the bishop's signature and authorizing her to open a shelter in San Diego. "I was caught with my pants down," the bishop commented later.

Mother Teresa exemplified wonderfully well what an

outstanding theologian, Karl Rahner (1904–84) wrote about human closeness to God: "the closer we are to God, the more our individual personality and freedom are enhanced." Unquestionably, Mother Teresa was very close to God. But that enhanced, rather than diminished, her freedom and personal characteristics.

Mother Teresa died in 1997, and John Paul II beatified her (declared her blessed and on the way to becoming a canonized saint) in October 2003 on a morning made fresh by overnight rain. Over one hundred thousand pilgrims and tourists attended the ceremony in St Peter's Square. Several hundred homeless people were seated near the altar and afterwards shared a lunch served by the diplomatic corps.

The media came in full force, partly to honour Mother Teresa and partly to use the occasion as a dry run for the coming death and funeral of John Paul II. On the BBC platform I was broadcasting with Brian Hanrahan, initiating a happy partnership with that TV presenter. (Two years later I was to join him repeatedly for the death of John Paul II and the conclave that elected Pope Benedict XVI.) After Mother Teresa had been declared "blessed," the Mass continued with the preparation of the gifts of bread and wine. Four lovely Indian ladies wearing saris and carrying lights began dancing up to the altar. Hanrahan turned to me and said: "Father O'Collins, some people don't like this." "Brian, that's their problem," I assured him. "This is India's day in the sun. And what's more, I'm sure Mother Teresa wants me to say how much she approves of what the Indian ladies are doing."

As Jesus says in John's Gospel, "the poor you have always

with you" (John 12:8). Through what she did with her life Mother Teresa added: "Don't just deplore this situation; do something yourself."

10
Geoffrey Robinson Chapman (1930–2010)

Geoff Chapman was flying a glider over Britain when he suddenly realized the importance of a phone call he had received earlier that day from a journalist-friend in Rome: the late Pope John XXIII had left a spiritual diary. Geoff hastily landed, caught the next available flight to Rome, tracked down the Italian executor, and on the spot signed up for the English-language rights—beating more famous publishers who turned up the next day.

Geoff had founded Geoffrey Chapman Ltd in England in 1957, followed a few years later by Geoffrey Chapman Australia. As a publisher his most famous coup was the signing which secured *The Journal of a Soul* by Pope (now St) John XXIII.

During the Second Vatican Council (1962–65), Geoff often stayed at the Hotel Columbus near St Peter's Square, wining and dining bishops, cardinals, and theological experts. He began a lifelong friendship with Archbishop Denis Hurley of Durban, a courageous champion in the anti-apartheid struggle and a leader in the reform of rites for worship.

For Geoff, the work the Council did towards updating the Catholic Church and promoting relations with other Christians was a dream come true. As soon as Vatican II ended, he published its sixteen (Latin) documents in an English translation, with introductions by Catholics and Protestants who had attended the four sessions of the Council as observers. The worldwide sales of this volume went up to a million copies.

Geoff's spectacular success did not always go down well. It prompted another, envious publisher into saying: "Jesus said that you can serve either God or Mammon. But Geoff has proved Jesus wrong. You can serve God *and* Mammon."

In 1969 Geoff and his wife, Sue, sold the Geoffrey Chapman imprint to Crowell, Collier and Macmillan, but continued to work for the firm until 1971. They then joined Collins Publishers, and the following year set up Collins Liturgical Publications. Using the new texts produced by the commissions working in the aftermath of Vatican II, they published Sunday and weekday missals, lectionaries, and breviaries for all the English-speaking world outside North America. They also supported and published for all Christian churches the *Australian Hymn Book* (1977), a major ecumenical achievement and a mega-seller for many years.

Born in Melbourne (Australia), Geoff grew up near Port Phillip Bay and quickly became expert at sailing. We were together at the Jesuit high school, Xavier College, but with a difference. I faced the rigours of being a boarder: cold showers each morning except Saturday; basic but unappetising food; and the absence of the emotional warmth and support of living at home. As a "dayboy," Geoff lived with his family in a delightful, bayside suburb and, despite facing a daily commute by train and tram to the school, enjoyed a privileged upbringing.

Part III: Friends

We arrived together at the University of Melbourne, where he studied law (1949–53), and honed his business skills. In 1954 he sailed for London with his bride Suzanne James, and three years later founded Geoffrey Chapman Ltd. Predictably this choice of city and profession evoked the memory of another couple: Frank Sheed (1897–1981) and Maisie Ward (1889–75).

Born in Australia and educated at the University of Sydney, after the end of World War I, Frank Sheed left for England and married Maisie Ward, the descendant of a distinguished English Catholic family. Maisie and Frank met through their work for the Catholic Evidence Guild. They were both forceful public speakers and became well reviewed authors, as well as outstanding publishers. In 1926 they founded Sheed & Ward, which published works by Hilaire Belloc, G. K. Chesterton, Ronald Knox, Evelyn Waugh and other notable writers, as well as issuing translations of some of the best French and German authors. Inevitably contemporaries of Geoff and Sue Chapman thought of them as a post-World War II couple who reaped and spread the harvest of Vatican II, which another couple, Frank Sheed and Maisie Ward, had earlier helped to prepare.

A genial, hard-working publisher, Geoff's many friends included Archbishop Desmond Tutu of South Africa. For the Anglicans of southern Africa, Geoff published a prayer book in twelve different languages; it was launched by Archbishop Tutu in May 1989.

Along with his passion for post-World War II theology coming out of Europe, and especially from France, Geoff became a skilful glider pilot. He also continued to polish his art as a yachtsman, which he had learnt as a boy. He competed twice for the Fastnet Challenge Cup off the south coast of England and Ireland.

For many years we lived in different cities and, normally, distant countries. While aware of each other's doings and sharing many friends, we met only once—when Geoff and Sue came to visit one of their children at the University of Cambridge in the early 1970s. But the break of many years did not matter. In 2006 I could reclaim my friendship with Geoff and Sue when I came to spend three years in a Jesuit community, a very short walk from their home in Wimbledon. Geoff was struggling with cancer but remained a person of robust faith and the incarnation of affability. We talked endlessly as the sun went down over Wimbledon.

Leaving for Melbourne the year before Geoff died, I could not attend his funeral. But Sue shared with me all the details. Shortly before he lapsed into his final coma, he murmured words from the medieval mystic Julian of Norwich: "All shall be well."

Geoff was survived by his wife Sue, six children, and twelve grand-children.

11
Fra' Richard Sydney Benedict Divall (1945–2017)

This portrait has three complementary panels: an obituary of Richard Divall that I have never before published, the homily I preached at his funeral Mass in St Patrick's Cathedral (Melbourne), and the homily I preached at an anniversary Mass a year later in the Chapel of the Holy Spirit, Newman College (University of Melbourne).

Obituary of Richard Divall

Richard Sydney Benedict Divall, who has died aged 71, was one of Australia's best loved conductors and teachers of music. A person of infectious enthusiasm and faith-driven kindness, Richard was never dull but always entertaining and well informed.

The son of Frederick Ronald and Dorothy Margaret Divall, Richard studied at the Sydney Conservatorium of Music and the University of Melbourne. He was awarded honorary doctorates from Monash University (Melbourne), the University of Sao Paolo (Brazil), and Australian Catholic University, as well as receiving an OBE (Order of the British Empire,1961), AO (Order of Australia, 2009), the Sir Bernard Heinze Award (2005), the Bayreuth Prize (1990), the Dame Joan Hammond Award (1988), and many other awards (including that of being named "outstanding Victorian" for 1993).

After nine years as a music program producer for the Australian Broadcasting Commission, from 1972, on the invitation of Dame Joan Hammond (1912–96), an internationally acclaimed operatic soprano notable for her Puccini roles, Richard became for twenty-five years Music Director of the Victorian State Opera, and for a further five years Principal Resident Conductor of Opera Australia. Those years became the golden age of opera in the State of Victoria. In 1984 he conducted Verdi's *Don Carlos*, the first opera to be staged in the newly built State Theatre of the Victorian Arts Centre. As well as conducting for concerts and ballets, from 1968 he conducted over 150 operas.

Richard continued conducting operas down to late 2015, with a celebrated production of Gaetano Donizetti's *Maria Stuarda*. He was preparing to conduct another Donizetti opera, *Anna Bolena*, in late 2016 but, debilitated by cancer, he passed the baton to a younger conductor and friend, Richard Mills. These two operas end with a dramatic beheading, the former with the execution of Mary Queen of Scots and the latter with that of Anne Boleyn. "Richard," I said to him, "you seem to have a taste for gory beheadings." But he delighted rather in the fierce clash between the two sopranos, in which Mary calls Elizabeth a "bastard" (*Maria Stuarda*).

For Richard the main thing was to do one's job with professional expertise and with loving respect for others. He took special delight in being chief adjudicator and conductor of the Herald-Sun Aria competition (1997–2015), which provided scholarships that regularly prepared young singers to sing at the Royal Opera House (London) and other leading venues around the world. He also assisted Allan and Maria Myers at their music festivals, a local Glyndebourne event staged at the Myers's estate, Dunkeld in the Western District of Victoria. For the centenary of the landing at Gallipoli (1915) in World War I, he collaborated with Lady Primrose Potter, the Ian Potter Foundation, Monash University, and the Returned Service League in producing an outstanding CD. It featured an elegy and four other works by Frederick Septimus Kelly, an Australian composer and friend of the poet Rupert Brooke. Present for Brooke's burial on the island of Skyros. Kelly was twice wounded at Gallipoli and died in 1916 in one of the last great battles of the Somme.

From 1991 Richard was an associate professor at the School of Music and from 2005 Principal Fellow of the Faculty of Music at the University of Melbourne. In 1977 he began a twenty-three-year stint as Artist-in-residence at Queen's College, University of Melbourne. In 2010 he became a Vice-Chancellor's Professorial Fellow at Monash University, and offered sell-out courses on conducting. In 2014 he taught an acclaimed course on conducting as Visiting Professor of Music at King's College, London, where his students won significant awards.

A precious milestone for Richard was his being received into the Catholic Church at St Patrick's Cathedral (Melbourne) in 1989. Bishop Kallistos Ware of Oxford University had encouraged him on that journey of faith. Richard's godparents were Sir James and Lady Shirley Gobbo. A Rhodes scholar, president of the Oxford boating union when they beat Cambridge in the centenary race of 1954, and Supreme Court judge, Gobbo would serve as Governor of the State of Victoria. Among those who attended the reception in the cathedral were Sister Fabian Wilhelmina Elliott (in her time the most famous nursing sister in Australia), Lady Potter, and Dame Joan Hammond.

Nearly thirty years later Lady Potter was to proclaim the first reading at Richard's requiem held in the same cathedral and attended by a thousand people, and Sir James gave the eulogy at the end of Mass.

By that time Dame Joan Hammond was long since dead. She had treasured for her own prayer life a large, antique set of rosary beads, and bequeathed them to Richard. Until his own death, Richard clung to those beads and wore them when formally dressed as a knight of Malta. They were there in his coffin when it was carried out of the cathedral for burial in the Melbourne General Cemetery.

Richard joined the Order of Malta in 1990, and in 2009, as Fra' Richard, became a fully professed knight, the only one in Australia and, for that matter, in the entire Southern Hemisphere. Richard treasured his membership in the Order of Malta, joining in pilgrimages with sick people to the shrine of Lourdes in France and visiting Montenegro in a successful search for the precious icon of the Virgin Mary (as Our Lady of Philerme) that had been in the possession of the Knights of Malta until the Napoleonic Wars.

Home in Melbourne, he was assiduous attending special celebrations of the Eucharist for the aged and sick at day-care centers and hospices around the city. For Richard, the ideal set before members of the Order of Malta to treat the sick and poor as nothing less than their "lords" was a lived reality. The sick and elderly felt cheered by the sight of Fra' Richard and other knights and dames of Malta who had dropped their regular work and come

Part III: Friends

in traditional robes to spend a morning with them. When driving to these events, Richard enthralled me with stories of Dame Joan Hammond, Sir Charles Mackerras, Luciano Pavarotti, Tito Gobbi, Katia Ricciarelli, and other "greats" in the story of modern music, or else filled his Peugeot with recordings of eighteenth-century sacred music from Malta and Naples.

Richard excelled in editing and publishing (after sometimes rediscovering) sacred and secular music from the UK, Malta, and Australia: for instance, the symphonies of Samuel Wesley; the complete works of Michael Christian Festing (died 1752 and a direct ancestor of the ex-Prince and Grand Master of the Order of Malta, Matthew Festing); and volumes of Maltese baroque music. Richard stood alone as a pioneering champion of the history of nineteenth- and early-twentieth century music in Australia (e.g. the musical works by the novelist Henry Handel Richardson). Richard prepared hundreds of editions, forty-five of which had been published electronically before his death by the Music Archives of Monash University, including works by Isaac Nathan, Charles Horsley, Fritz Hart, Frederick Septimus Kelly and G. W. Marshall-Hall. Those publications form a lasting monument to what Richard achieved for the history of music in Australia and beyond. A dear and internationally renowned friend, Professor John Griffiths, will ensure that the rest of the editions prepared by Richard will also be published.

When I returned to Melbourne in 2009, I decided not to accept any more doctoral candidates. At the Gregorian University (Rome) I had supervised ninety-two successful dissertations, and that seemed enough. Now Richard wanted to write and earn a doctorate (at the University of Divinity) and already had his topic: the sacred music of a Maltese composer, Nicolò Isouard (1773–1818). But I could not take on the supervision without the support of an expert musicologist. John Griffiths, a bearded specialist in sixteenth-century Spanish music, stepped forward, and we stood proudly alongside Richard when he received the doctorate in 2013. It made Richard the world expert on Isouard.

With his warm, attractive, and amusing personality and constant net-working, Richard enjoyed endless friends and admirers. He never allowed himself to be crushed by the onset of cancer in 2010. I lived only a short distance from his home. He became for me what he was for so many others—a wonderful human presence and spiritual blessing.

After one operation, when Richard moved to the rehabilitation floor of another hospital, I came to anoint him and bring him Holy Communion. A dear friend and patron with wonderful eyelashes, the slim, elegant, widowed Lady Primrose Potter, happened to be in a room right opposite his, undergoing rehabilitation for a hip replacement. With simple, edifying devotion they both received the anointing of the sick and Communion, prayed in silence for a few minutes, and then broke out the champagne they had slipped into the hospital.

Richard is survived by his sister Susan, his brother Kenneth, and many treasured friends. May this marvellous person rest in peace with God!

Part III: Friends

Homily for the Requiem Mass (January 25, 2017)

"Mary Magdalene announced to the disciples: 'I have seen the Lord'" (John 20:18).

My dear friends, at the birth of Christianity, Mary Magdalene was the first and the greatest witness to Jesus risen from the dead. She ran from the tomb to share with the other disciples the unique good news that would turn their lives around: Jesus, who had been crucified and buried, had gloriously risen from the dead. Alleluia! When Christianity began, Mary Magdalene showed herself a unique Easter person, an Alleluia person.

Two thousand years later, our dear friend Richard Divall proved himself to be nothing less than a remarkable Easter person, an Alleluia person who blessed so many institutions and so many individuals. He was a blessing to the Order of Malta, to the Australian String Quartet family, Orchestra Victoria, the Royal Melbourne Philharmonic, the Melbourne Symphony Orchestra, and other orchestras; a blessing to Newman College and Queen's College within the University of Melbourne; to Catholic Theological College within the University of Divinity; a blessing to the choir of St Francis Church and other churches and cathedrals in Australia; a blessing to the Ian Potter Foundation, to the University of Melbourne, King's College London, Monash University and other universities where students took his sell-out courses in conducting; a blessing to the Dunkeld Festival and to the Herald-Sun Aria competition; a blessing to the ABC as music program producer; and a blessing to the State Library Victoria, to Victoria State Opera, Victorian Opera, Melbourne Opera and further operatic companies by his extraordinary contribution to the production of operas. It was Richard who was primarily responsible for blessing the State of Victoria with a golden age of operas. Yes, Richard was an Easter person who gave direction and vitality to numerous institutions.

But he was also an Easter person who gave fresh life to countless individuals. Very many of you present this morning could tell stories of Richard proving a grace and blessing in your own lives. When you remember his voice and see again his smile, so many of you will simply say, "Alleluia! What a life-giving blessing he was to me!" He proved a blessing not only through his generous and tireless help but also by sharing with others his spirit of thanksgiving. Richard was a deeply grateful person, who often said, "Thank you *so much*."

Richard had a remarkable eye and ear for young singers and performers. He had a delight in helping aspiring artists find their way in the careers that opened up to them. He was a mentor, friend and inspiration for many other young people—not least the students of Newman College and Queen's College.

In recalling Richard's care for individuals, one must not forget what he did for the homeless, the old, and the dying. On winter evenings, along with other members of the Order of Malta, he would be out on the Melbourne streets to talk with the homeless and bring them a thick coat to keep them warm. Over and over again, with other knights and dames of Malta, he visited the sick and the aged in retirement homes and day-care centres. Yes, Richard was a truly outstanding conductor, a remarkable teacher of music, and a pioneering editor of musical works. But he never failed to be a life-giving person, an Easter person, to so many individuals, young and old, rich and poor.

We have all seen classic paintings of the risen Christ appearing to Mary Magdalene, and felt the unique Easter joy expressed by those works of art. Let me finish with three joyful pictures of Richard. The first comes from the Hamer Hall on October 26, 2016, the final evening of the last Herald-Sun Aria competition. When his young friend Alexander Ross pushed Richard in a wheelchair onto the stage to receive a present, the applause was electrifying. It was the wider, Victorian audience saying thank you and goodbye to a cherished friend. The second picture is from a dinner at the Athenaeum Club two weeks later on November 11— a kind of Last Supper at which Richard's beaming face spread joy everywhere. The final picture comes from Caritas Christi hospice, a few days before he died, when he lay in bed clasping the rosary beads which Dame Joan Hammond had left to him. We prayed together. As I was leaving, I said to Richard: "we are *all* in God's hands." "Yes," he replied, "we *are* all in God's hands, and *that* is the best place to be." Richard, thank you *so much*. You were a remarkable Easter person, a real Alleluia person, who enriched us all. Richard, thank you *so much*.

Homily for the Mass in Memory of Richard Divall, January 25, 2018.

Today's feast, the conversion of St Paul, is filled with the joy of the resurrection of Jesus. The reading from the Book of Acts has described how Paul was dramatically changed by meeting Jesus risen from the dead. A ruthless persecutor of the first Christians, Paul was transformed into a great apostle of the risen Jesus. In the language of the Gospel [Mark 16:15–18], Paul went out into the whole, known world and preached the good news of Easter. Death could not put an end to Jesus. He rose from the dead and all things were filled with new life. Alleluia. That was the person Paul met on the road to Damascus. That was the person whose message Paul began to preach: the wonderfully beautiful Jesus who can fill our hearts with the deepest joy now and forever.

What the resurrection of Christ promises us is that the world to which we go is no grey haunt of ghosts. It will bring a totally satisfying existence in which we will know the gloriously beautiful Christ and all our dear ones, and be known by them. We have the Lord's promise: 'If I go and prepare a place for you, I shall come again and take you to myself, so that where I am, there you also may be.'

It is year since Richard Divall left us for eternal life. By this time, Richard has certainly met St Paul. Now I don't know what they said when first they met. My guess is that Paul may have thanked Richard for being such powerful witness to the resurrection of Jesus. Richard was an Easter person, an Alleluia person. He believed in Jesus risen from the dead. And Richard acted on his Easter faith. He helped any number of people rise above deadly situations, and find new hope. Music is the language of the heart. Richard spoke that language, and shared with others the Easter life and joy that filled his heart.

When we think of Richard, we think of operas, perhaps one of those more than 150 operas he conducted during his lifetime. The beauty of operas can lift and open us to the mysterious beauty of the crucified and risen Jesus. Richard spent many years immersed in operatic beauty, a beauty which can transform us by bringing the new life and hope that comes through tragic death.

Very many people present here this morning will have stories to tell about Richard, stories of a warm, attractive human personality but also stories of a true Easter person. In a superb obituary of Richard published last year in *The Australian*, Richard Mills drew it all together with a phrase from the Latin text of the Creed: "*et expecto resurrectionem mortuorum* (I look forward to the resurrection of the dead)." It's a thrilling phrase that resonates in our memories with the classical musical settings of the Creed. It's a phrase that also resonates with and sums up the life of Richard Divall. He showed the Easter joy of someone who loved Jesus risen from the dead and, like St Paul, looked forward to the resurrection of the dead. For Richard and for St Paul, what ultimately mattered was the Lord's promise: "If I go and prepare a place for you, I shall come again and take you to myself, so that where I am, you also may be."

12
Prince Frank Pogson Doria Pamphij (1923–1998)

It was no accident that I first met Frank and Orietta Pogson Doria Pamphilj through a young American who was writing his thesis with me. The priest belonged to those generations of students who came from all round the world to study in Rome and enjoyed a delicious surprise: the relaxed and unassuming friendship of Frank and his marvellous wife. To borrow the language of the great Bengali poet, Rabindranath Tagore (1861–1941), many who briefly visited the eternal city or stayed for years could say to the Dorias: "I came as a stranger; you received me as a guest; and now I am departing as a friend." The Dorias had met the young American very simply. In a Roman *trattoria* they saw him dining by himself, and invited him to join them.

Year by passing year, the Christmas carols in the Palazzo Doria were vividly memorable occasions when Frank and Orietta brought together family and friends around the piano in their home. Led by a student from the Venerable English College, we had to sing our way through a booklet of carols before being allowed to move on to supper. At buffet meals, I frequently gravitated toward Frank, unless first summoned there by his incomparable butler, Mario.

Dapper and slightly ruddy in complexion, Frank was always happy to talk about his years at sea during the Second World War: on convoys in the North Atlantic and then mine-sweeping in the Adriatic. Courageous man that he was, he never spoke of the dangers he had faced, but recalled the friends he made in the armed forces. He was always a great teaser, and joked about my persistent failure to distinguish between being "in" a ship and "on" a ship. I never knew Frank to tell set-piece jokes. But he inserted brilliantly funny remarks into conversations going on around him.

He could also laugh at himself. When we were rehearsing his daughter's wedding in the Doria church, St Agnes on the Piazza Navona, the short aisle meant that he walked her from the door to the altar in a minute or so. "Frank, let's have the entrance march again," I told him. "You'll have to take it more slowly with Gesine." With a smile he excused himself: "I'm trying to get rid of her quickly. Can't you see that?"

Frank grew up Anglican, was received into the Catholic Church, and remained ecumenical through and through. He and Orietta regularly attended the major, public lecture at the Gregorian University that leading Anglican, Orthodox, and Protestant scholars delivered as part of their duties as visiting professors. George Lindbeck from the USA, Bishop Eduard Lohse from Germany, James Dunn from the UK, and the others were normally surprised and delighted to find the Prince and Princess Doria following their lecture from the front row and greeting them afterwards.

Part III: Friends

Memory brings back many pictures of him, always surrounded by family and friends. If anyone deserved the title of a "people's person," it was Frank. The people extended beyond his loving family to old colleagues from World War II, bishops and students, distinguished scholars, Italians of all kinds, the English-speaking colony in Rome, diplomats and other visitors from outside Italy, right through to small children. One of my last memories of him is his warm welcome to little Abigail, an eleven-year-old American on her first visit to Rome with her parents.

From early 1997, when a heart condition meant that Frank could only move around in a wheelchair, I started coming each week to say the Sunday Mass for him and Orietta in their sitting room. "You are the specialist in St Paul," I told him, and always asked him to take the second reading, which regularly came from the apostle's letters. From his wheelchair he proclaimed Paul's words with care and concentration. His quiet devotion touched me again and again. Then in the minutes after Communion when the three of us, sometimes joined by visitors, sat in silence gave me a fresh sense of how we experience the communion of saints in the presence of the risen Christ.

For me and for so many others, Frank was love, loyalty, friendship, and fun personified. He was all that for his wife, their children, Jonathan and Gesine, his sister Margaret, and the rest of the family. At his death a Catholic weekly, the London *Tablet*, lost a great friend and supporter, and so did many in Rome. I think of Mario and his wife, of Frank's incredibly competent nurse Annette, or her student daughter Clarissa, and others who made up the village which was the historic center of Rome.

After years of struggling with ill health, our friend Frank went off to heaven. We mourned his passing, gave thanks for his life, and knew that we would be merry with him together when home with our God.

13
Princess Orietta Pogson Doria Pamphilj (1922–2000)

The tall daughter and only child of a Doria prince and a Scottish mother, Princess Orietta Doria Pamphilj inherited the patrimony of one of Italy's greatest family. One ancestor was Admiral Andrea Doria, the mastermind of the Christian victory over the Turkish fleet at the Battle of Lepanto (1571). Another ancestor was Giambattista Pamphilj, who became Innocent X (pope 1644–55). His famous portrait by Velázquez hangs in the Galleria Doria in Rome.

It was after the liberation of Rome in June 1944 that she first met the English naval officer Frank Pogson whom she was to marry. He had docked his minesweeper in Ancona, where she came to work in a canteen as a volunteer for the Catholic Women's League. She had just emerged from hiding out in Rome with her parents during the Nazi occupation of the city. "The most wonderful sight in my life was a young American soldier I saw the morning we came out of hiding," she told me. "He was exhausted and asleep in the sun on top of his tank in the Piazza Venezia."

Months earlier when German soldiers raided the Doria Palace, Prince Filippo Andrea, Princess Gesine, and their daughter Orietta hid in a lavatory behind a sliding bookcase listening to the soldiers clumping around the gigantic building. After the soldiers left, the Dorias slipped away through the night across the Tiber. The parish priest of Santa Maria in Trastevere hid them for months and shared his food (mainly vegetables) with them. Everyone went very hungry and lived in constant fear.

Orietta's father, the Prince Doria, continued working secretly with a Vatican monsignor, Hugh O'Flaherty, a Scarlet Pimpernel figure who organized hiding places and food for thousands of escaped Allied POWs, Jews, and others on the run from the enemy forces. In 1943–44 there was a high price on the Prince's head. "*The Scarlet and the Black* dramatized things," Orietta admitted. "But it really caught the feeling of those dreadful months, when Herbert Kappler killed people or deported them to Auschwitz." In the film Sir John Gielgud appeared as Pius XII, Gregory Peck as O'Flaherty, and Christopher Plummer as the ruthless Colonel Kappler.

Born in 1922, Orietta divided her schooling between Rome, England, and Switzerland. Her father's chronically poor health involved a long stay in the Swiss mountains with his wife and daughter (1938–39). In Switzerland Orietta developed her love for mountaineering and skiing. Her education may have been fragmented, but she grew up speaking excellent French as well as English and Italian.

Orietta had a great affinity with her father. When Prince Filippo came out of hiding in June 1944, the Allied authorities appointed him mayor of Rome. He led the city well until democratic elections could once again be held. Orietta shared his sense of service. She handled motor vehicles with skill, and from the 1940s until the end of her life had a truck driver's licence. That licence also let her drive vehicles for the girl guides, an organization that she supported with energy and generosity.

When she married Frank in 1958, her father had given his full blessing to their union but, sadly, died a few months before the wedding took place. Mean-minded gossips among the Roman nobility falsely suggested that Prince Filippo opposed the marriage—something that in any case he was unlikely to do, since he had married a Scottish nurse and was related to the Dukes of Newcastle and the Earls of Shrewsbury. Orietta felt deeply let down by the gossip coming from the Roman families, some of whom had compromised themselves by earlier accepting the fascist regime of Mussolini.

In any case Orietta had the strength and wisdom to adapt to the post-war world, which was very different from the one in which she had been raised as the only child of an immensely rich, aristocratic family that spent the summers in the Villa Doria Pamphilj on the top of the Janiculum and the winters in their 1,000-room palace at the heart of Old Rome. She could never identify with the nobility who pretended that everything had remained just the same. One only needed to see Orietta riding her bicycle around the city or hear her talk with shopkeepers to realize how she identified with ordinary people.

She never agreed with the post-war critics who attacked Pope

Pius XII for deciding that it would be counter-productive for him to denounce publicly the Nazi genocidal persecution of the Jews.[31] The Dutch bishops spoke out strongly, and the Nazis reacted by deporting from Holland more Jews and killing them in Auschwitz. Yet Orietta had little time for some who worked later in the Vatican. "They're a dreadful lot," she remarked to me more than once.

She and Frank, both devout Catholics with a life of daily prayer, gave strong support to inter-church relations when Pope John XXIII called the Second Vatican Council (1962–65). In their other palace overlooking the Piazza Navona, they made available a meeting place for non-Catholic observers who attended the Council. Part of that palace became Foyer Unitas, a residence for non-Catholic visitors administered with skill and devotion by the Ladies of Bethany. The Franciscan Friars of the Atonement were welcomed, and continue to run there the Centro Pro Unione, one of the world's most successful ecumenical study-centers.

On the Via del Corso, the Palazzo Doria itself came to house the Anglican Centre, the fruit of a 1966 meeting between Pope Paul VI and the Archbishop of Canterbury, Dr Michael Ramsey. When Ramsey's successor, Archbishop Robert Runcie visited Rome in 1989 and met John Paul II, Orietta and Frank offered Runcie a wonderful reception in their home. The Archbishop's visit to the pope outraged the Reverend Ian Paisley who descended on the city. On the evening of the Doria reception, he stood across the Corso

---

[31] See David Dalin, *The Myth of Hitler's Pope* (Washington, DC: Regnery, 2005). In making a strong case for Pius XII, Palin, a Jewish professor of history and political science, drew on many sources, but, surprisingly, did not use the Anglican historian Owen Chadwick, *Britain and the Vatican During the Second World War* (Cambridge, UK: Cambridge University Press, 1986). Among other things, that work documents how in the winter of 1939/40 Pius XII became involved with two leading German generals in a plot against Hitler.

from the palace door and held up a placard with a suitably anti-papal message.

Orietta was a Roman to the core. One memorable Sunday she and Frank joined me for a day or prayer out at Villa Cavalletti in the Alban Hills. When we drove back to Rome, turned a corner on the Via Quattro Novembre and came down the hill towards the Piazza Venezia, I felt a little bump. "That hole has been there since the war," Orietta explained. She cherished her city right down to minor potholes and the memory of the shuffling sound of sheep being driven at night down the Via del Corso.

Orietta and Frank were a great twosome; his sense of fun checked her tendency to over-seriousness. After she underwent a serious operation in the Roman hospital of Salvator Mundi, I came one afternoon, found her alone, and blurted out something that I had been waiting to say for years: "I find it very touching to see how much Frank loves you and misses you right now." In her usual matter-of-fact style, she brushed my remark aside but could not help letting me see how I had caught the heart of her existence.

For years the prayerful princess struggled against cancer with cheerful courage and never a hint of self-pity. She was survived by her children, grandchildren, a butler *par excellence*, his wife who cooked with such skill, and so many other friends who formed the Doria village at the historic heart of old Rome.

Only a month before she died, Orietta was invested by Her Majesty Queen Elizabeth with an OBE (Order of the British Empire) and a few hours later attended the pre-lunch drinks party for the Queen held in the Anglican Centre, now housed in splendid new quarters above the Doria Gallery. It was Orietta's final and most fitting public appearance.

In October 2000 twelve priests concelebrated her funeral Mass, including the rector of the Beda College, the rector of the Scots College, and the acting rector of the English College—fittingly, for those colleges were very dear to Orietta. The chief celebrant was her childhood friend, Bishop Luigi del Gallo di Roccagiovine. He preached in Italian and I preached in English. The basilica of the Dodici Apostoli was packed. Afterwards I buried Orietta in the family chapel, up in the grounds of the Villa Doria Pamphilj, in a tomb right next to Frank's. In the Doria village at the heart of old Rome, along with many others, I felt that we had lost our "mum."

14
Cardinal Avery Dulles (1918–2008)

A final lecture delivered by Cardinal Avery Dulles offered a moving testimony to his life as a theologian and Jesuit. "There is no one on earth with whom I would want to exchange places," he said. "It has been a special privilege to serve in the Society of Jesus, a religious community specially dedicated to the Savior of the world."

When he gave that lecture, Cardinal Dulles was already stricken with health problems, the long term result from an attack of polio suffered when serving in the American navy during the Second World War. Since 1988, he had occupied the McGinley Chair in theology at the Jesuit-run Fordham University in the Bronx, New York. The previous thirty-eight McGinley Lectures had already been published in a handsome volume which he presented to Pope Benedict XVI on his April 2008 visit to the United States.

By the time Avery delivered the thirty-ninth lecture, he was becoming increasingly disabled, yet he remarked: "I can identify with the paralytic and mute persons in the Gospels, grateful for the loving and skilful care I receive and for the hope of everlasting life in Christ. The Lord now calls me to a period of weakness. I know well that his power can be made perfect in weakness." The period lasted only a few months. He reached his ninetieth birthday on August 24 and died on the morning of December 12.

The son of John Foster Dulles, Secretary of State under President Dwight Eisenhower, Avery was raised in the Presbyterian Church and did his undergraduate studies at Harvard University. He became desperate to know whether there was anything worth living or dying for. As he explained in *A Testimonial to Grace*, that desperation led him through ancient Greek philosophy to the Catholic Church, which he joined in 1940. Conscious of the emptiness of life based on the pursuit of pleasure, he had come to see that happiness is the reward for holding to what is "truly good and important."

In 1946 Avery entered the Society of Jesus and completed his studies with a doctorate in 1960 at the Gregorian University in Rome. There he met Jacques Dupuis, and years later contributed a chapter to *In Many and Various Ways*, a volume published for Dupuis's eightieth birthday in 2003. Specializing in the areas of divine revelation and the Church, Avery taught at Woodstock College in Maryland (moved later to New York) and at Catholic University of America in Washington, DC, before settling finally in Fordham.

He was also a visiting professor at many academic centers, including the Gregorian University and Oxford University where his Martin D'Arcy Lectures appeared as *The Catholicity of the Church* in 1985. In Catholic theology, Avery pioneered the use of models, or elaborated images, in two landmark books: *Models of the Church* (1974) and *Models of Revelation* (1983). Before publishing the latter book, he sent the manuscript to me for suggestions and corrections. I had some to make, but regretted later failing to propose more attention to the public worship of Christians, a major way in which divine self-revelation continues to reach millions of believers.

It was shortly after I arrived for the first time in the United States that I met Avery. Fresh from my doctorate studies at the University of Cambridge, I came to Weston School of Theology in Cambridge, Massachusetts as a visiting professor to teach in the fall of 1968. Avery preached at the Mass of the Holy Spirit with which Weston School began its academic year. During the concelebrated Eucharistic Prayer, it happened that Avery said the prayer for the dead. When he paused for a few moments in silence, I knew he was praying for his father, the Secretary of State whose high-minded but rigid policies it had become popular to deride. Avery once told me of a dinner that his father gave for Charles Lindbergh in the hope of finding out whether the famous aviator really was a fascist. But right from our first meal together at the Midget, a Cambridge restaurant commemorated in Eric Segal's *Love Story*, we mainly talked theology. Avery put matters flatteringly: "I want to milk you for your theological ideas."

Over the years Avery was often with me in Rome, and I was sometimes with him in Washington, DC. In January 2002, after preaching for a week at the noon Mass in St Patrick's Church in downtown Washington, I joined him at the Feast of the Epiphany to celebrate a mega-Mass for the John Carroll Society.[32] The members included lawyers, doctors, judges, business people, one

---

[32] John Carroll SJ (1735–1815), Archbishop of Baltimore, was the first Catholic bishop in the United States and founder (1789) of Georgetown University, the oldest Catholic institution of higher learning in the United States.

or two members of President George W. Bush's administration, and others. I preached at the Mass; Avery, who had flown down from New York, presided at the Mass and afterwards spoke to the four hundred people at the brunch. Over the meal, Avery and I were presented with John Carroll Society Medals—a lovely gesture that I had not anticipated.

Tall, gaunt, and courageous, Avery had an infectious chuckle, a loyal love of friends, and, eventually, a conservative streak in his theology. A deep integrity shone out of him. He made no fuss when I invited him to join others in celebrating the life and work of Dupuis, even though the Congregation for the Doctrine of the Faith had issued a "notification" warning readers about "ambiguities" in Dupuis's *Toward a Christian Theology of Religious Pluralism*.[33] "I've read it twice," Avery told me, "and can't see what's wrong with it."

After twenty years on the Lutheran-Roman Catholic Dialogue in the United States, seven years as a consultor to the Secretariat for Dialogue with Non-Believers, and five years on the International Theological Commission, Avery's work for the Church and the world was fully recognized when Pope John Paul II created him a cardinal in 2001.

"Uncle Avery," as I spoke of him to others, was always a delightful companion. Once on a drive around Washington, we were deep into theological discussion when I reminded him that the car had previously belonged to his uncle, Alan Dulles, the first civilian director of the Central Intelligence Agency and its longest serving director (1952–61). "The Russians may have bugged this car," I suggested. "Don't worry," Avery retorted, "they won't understand

---

[33] Maryknoll, NY: Orbis Books, 1997.

a word of what we've been saying." Years later, in the aftermath of 9/11, airport security insisted that he take off his boots, which he had to wear because of the long-term effects of polio. "Doesn't bother you?," I asked. "Not much," he told me. "I always bring a long shoehorn with me."

In July 2008, when I visited him in the infirmary of Fordham University, he was no longer able to speak. I held his hands, and told him how much I and others treasured his work and loved him. He nodded toward a copy of his McGinley Lectures, a final gift to me. Before leaving, I fell to my knees and asked: "May I have your blessing?" He nodded agreement, struggled to raise his hand, and blessed me.

15
Jacques Dupuis, SJ (1923–2004)

I first met Jacques Dupuis early in 1971 when I spent several weeks teaching alongside him in India at a Jesuit theological college (St Mary's, Kurseong) near Darjeeling, where he had been a professor of theology since 1959. One of the seriously beautiful places in the world, Kurseong enjoys astounding views across rich forests and tea plantations as far as the majesty of Kanchenjunga, rising to 28,000 feet.

Besides his work in teaching theology, Dupuis helped Tibetan and other refugees living along the frontier of India. A luminous intelligence shone through the glasses perched on his oval face. Wiry and tireless, despite bouts of bad health, he was most energetically hospitable. On our free days he took me out to meet a wide variety of people: the monks at a high-altitude Buddhist monastery; the Dalai Lama's sister-in-law who was running a self-help refugee camp; and Sherpa Tensing, who shared in 1953 the first proven ascent of Mount Everest. As Dupuis raced his Yugoslavian motorbike along the narrow roads of the Himalayan foothills, I clung to him for dear life and prayed not to fall down the sheer precipices so close to our wheels.

When his theological college shifted to Delhi later in 1971, Dupuis made a 2,000-kilometre trip on his motorcycle right across northern India to his new home. There he became the chief theological adviser to the Bishops' Conference of India.

Born in Belgium in 1923, Dupuis grew up during the Second World War when German forces occupied his country. He joined the Society of Jesus in 1941 and seven years later realized his dream when superiors sent him to Calcutta. He came to know, admire, and love India profoundly, with its bountiful culture and spirituality. Altogether he spent thirty-six years there and used to say: "My exposure to the Indian reality has been the greatest grace I have received from God as far as my vocation as a theologian and professor is concerned." That exposure made him reflect long and sensitively on a theme that would appear in the teaching of Pope John Paul II: the activity of the Holy Spirit in the cultures and religions of the world.

At the invitation of René Latourelle, the dean of the theological faculty of the Gregorian University (Rome), Dupuis came to the Gregorian twice as a visiting professor. Then in 1984 he was transferred permanently to Rome. He quickly made his mark as a first-rate teacher in the second-cycle (master's) program in theology. His classes on the doctrine of Christ and Christ and other religions regularly drew more than two hundred students. They also sought him out in large numbers to direct their dissertations.

In India, Dupuis had been for twelve years editor of *Vidyajyoti, Journal of Theological Reflection*. In 1985 he took on the editorship of a quarterly, the *Gregorianum*, and for eighteen years did that job—again with professional skill. In Rome he also served for ten years

(1985–95) as a consultor of the Pontifical Council for Interreligious Dialogue and made a major contribution to its 1991 document *Dialogue and Proclamation*. As an interpreter he attended four of the bishops' synods held in Rome (1974, 1983, 1985, and 1987), and published in *Doctrine and Life* and elsewhere a remarkably detailed and insightful article on the dramatic 1974 synod and its theme: evangelisation. As one of the most significant post-Vatican II documents, I included this article by Dupuis as an appendix to my *Living Vatican II: The 21st Council for the 21st Century*.[34]

By 2003 the bibliography of the books, articles, and reviews published by Dupuis ran to forty pages. A tireless reader and writer, he made a monumental contribution with *The Christian Faith*, a collection of major doctrinal statements of the Catholic Church, which he originally edited with a colleague (Josef Neuner) and then edited alone. The work grew from 711 pages in the first (1973) edition to 1,135 pages in the seventh edition of 2001. It is an essential resource for anyone interested in studying seriously the two thousand years of the Church's official teaching.

His 447-page book, *Toward a Christian Theology of Religious Pluralism*[35], is the other most notable monument in the theological work of Dupuis. It was translated into five other languages, won a prize from the Catholic Press Association of America, and was evaluated in well over one hundred reviews. It is hard to think of any other work published after the Second Vatican Council which sparked off so much discussion in print and at conferences. But the book also plunged him into several years of deeply distressing controversy with the Congregation for the Doctrine of the Faith (CDF). After thirty-two months of investigation the CDF published

---

[34] Mahwah, NJ: Paulist Press, 2006.
[35] Maryknoll, NY: Orbis Books, 1997.

a "notification" in February 2001, which said that the book contained misleading "ambiguities" on certain "important points" (left unspecified), but did not charge him with doctrinal or theological error, nor require him to add or change a single word in his original text.

In *On the Left Bank of the Tiber*[36] I tell the whole, sordid story of the controversy between Dupuis and the CDF. Five years later, I still have not received a single challenge to anything I wrote about the controversy.

Some critics of Dupuis challenged his calling Christ the unique, universal and decisive Savior and Redeemer but not applying here the adjectives "absolute" and "definitive." Dupuis disliked the inflationary use of "absolute," which flourishes in much ordinary speech and some theological talk. He also maintained a line that goes back through Pope Paul VI to St Thomas Aquinas: only God, who is utterly necessary and unlimited, is truly absolute.

While he never wanted to reduce Christ to one savior among many, Dupuis recognized the limits involved in the incarnation of the Son of God, the limits affecting the created character of the human condition he assumed and of his human redemptive actions. Moreover, the incarnation was a free act of God's love and not unconditionally necessary. As regards God's self-revelation in Jesus Christ, Dupuis did not emphasize the fullness of that redemption to the point of ignoring "the glorious manifestation of our" Lord still to come (1 Timothy 6:14) and "the fullness of truth" which will only then appear.[37]

God writes straight with crooked lines. The controversy with

---

[36] Brisbane/Leominster: Connor Court/Gracewing, 2013.
[37] John Paul II, *Fides et Ratio* (1998 encyclical on faith and reason), art. 2.

the CDF led to invitations for lectures right across Europe and in other parts of the world. In 2001 Dupuis delivered the *Tablet* lecture, on "Christianity and Other Religions: From Confrontation to Dialogue" (published in three parts in October-November 2001). His rich experience in India had made this topic the top project for his life's work. In the aftermath of the Second Vatican Council and the terrorist attacks of September 11, 2001, Dupuis had seen dialogue with other religions take its rightful place among the key questions of our day.

The title for a volume honouring him on his eightieth birthday, *In Many and Various Ways*,[38] came from the opening words of the Letter to the Hebrews. It reflects the question with which Dupuis grappled for more than fifty years: the mystery of God's one but complex plan to call all people through the Incarnate Word and the Holy Spirit to share forever in the divine life. Two cardinals (Avery Dulles and Franz König) and two archbishops contributed to the volume, along with other notable scholars.

A year later, even though his health had deteriorated, Dupuis celebrated in December 2004 the fiftieth anniversary of his ordination to the priesthood. Two days after Christmas he suffered a cerebral haemorrhage and died in hospital the following day, December 28, the feast of the Holy Innocents.

William Burrows, the managing editor of Orbis Books and publisher of Dupuis's major works, had this to say on the occasion of his eightieth birthday: "Jacques Dupuis has been at the forefront of Catholic theological efforts to explore the implications of the Second Vatican Council and its positive reappraisal of the status of 'other' religious traditions." When Dupuis died, I received the

---

[38] Maryknoll, NY: Orbis, 2003.

following message from Burrows: "Jacques was a great man in a small body. The more I worked with him, the clearer it became that his personality in its deepest recesses had been formed by the Spiritual Exercises of St Ignatius. He attempted to say 'Yes' to Christ in everything he did, all the while practising 'thinking with the Church.'"

Because of that fidelity to Christ and the Church, Dupuis found the accusations against him so disconcerting. May the Lord have long ago healed those wounds and taken Jacques to himself in everlasting light.

"Peacemaker between the World's Religions"
by John Wilkins, The Tablet, July 11, 2015.

"There can be no peace among the nations", Hans Küng has said, "without peace among the religions; and no peace among the religions without dialogue between the religions." Easier said than done, judging by the storm of controversy that broke around the Belgian Jesuit Jacques Dupuis at the turn of the millennium. *The Tablet* is no stranger to controversy, and found itself playing an active part.

Anyone who met Dupuis was conscious that here was a human being of exceptional luminous intelligence. That face I remember so well looks out from the photographs: oval shaped, large dark-framed glasses befitting an intellectual, serious, a lurking touch of sardonic humour. He had little time for small talk. When thinking – and Jacques was always thinking – he was very much a man alone.

In India, where he spent 36 years – "the greatest grace I received from God", he would say – he was a revered teacher and adviser to the bishops. In 1984 he transferred to the Gregorian University in Rome, Jesuit-run, where his classes drew several hundred students.

Then in 1997 he published his masterpiece, *Toward a Christian Theology of Religious Pluralism*, developing his thesis that the other world religions were present not just de facto but de iure, as an intended part of God's plan for the salvation of the human race in which they have their own role to play. And now very soon he was in trouble. In India his approach had been considered by some colleagues to be too conservative. In Rome it was thought too radical.

On 10 June 1998 a plenary meeting of the Congregation for the Doctrine of the Faith (CDF) decided to file an investigation, finding "grave errors and doctrinal ambiguities" in the book. Dupuis was devastated in October when 14 critical theses reached him from the congregation via the Jesuit General, Peter-Hans Kolvenbach. His loyalty to the Church was total. For it to be called in question was more than he could bear, and he had to go to hospital – the first of several visits.

His best friend in Rome, the Australian Gerald O'Collins, supported him from the start. The two Jesuits had first met in India in 1971. A highly respected theologian working creatively and productively in the central avenues of the Christian faith, O'Collins was one of the closest editorial advisers to *The Tablet* and a frequent contributor to its pages. I published his review of Dupuis' book in the issue of 24 January 1998. It was "superb", O'Collins thought, heralding "a profound shift in the Christian understanding of other religions".

One of those who read that review was the emeritus Archbishop of Vienna, Franz König, a senior cardinal who had been one of the pillars of the achievement of the Second Vatican Council.

Interreligious dialogue had fascinated him from his youth. He ordered the book at once, and "devoured" it (his word). He scribbled pencilled comments in the margins, and in addition piled up a wad of notes inside the cover.

When he learned of the action against Dupuis, he was highly disturbed. The correspondent for *The Tablet* in Vienna, Christa Pongratz-Lippitt, König's trusted aide and confidante, has recorded in her diary how several times he asked her to come round and see him. She found him "a changed man". On each occasion, instead of remaining calmly seated as he usually did, he would stride up and down. He occasionally interrupted the discussion to ask her to wait while he went to his study to telephone Rome. Once when he came back "he was very pale, and when he picked up a book his hand shook – something I had never seen before nor ever experienced again." It transpired that he had been in touch with the CDF authorities, and had found they had never studied the book deeply.

Through Christa, König asked me if he could defend Dupuis in *The Tablet*. The article he wrote for the issue of January 16, 1999 took the CDF to task head-on. "One should surely be able to rely on the doctrinal congregation to find better ways of doing its job... My heart bleeds when I see such obvious harm being done to the common good of God's Church... The Congregation for the Doctrine of the Faith has moved too fast too soon."

The prefect of the CDF, Joseph Ratzinger (later Benedict XVI), felt impelled to reply. He wrote to Cardinal König and sent me an English translation with an invitation to publish it. Headlined "An Open Letter", it appeared in *The Tablet* for March 13, 1999. "It was with astonishment and some sadness that I read your article", he told König. He asked: "Is dialogue with authors to be forbidden to us? Is the attempt to reach confidential clarification on difficult questions something evil? Is it not rather a way of striving to serve in a positive way the further development of faith and theology?"

Dupuis had responded to the CDF's enquiries with two sets of answers running to some 200 and 60 pages respectively. I published several editorials backing him. But the matter was moving inexorably towards a showdown. The locus classicus is the memoir by Gerry O'Collins, entitled *On the Left Bank of the Tiber*. In the relevant chapter, its author, known for his unfailing good humour and fair judgement, shows flashes of real anger. "Dupuis' skirmish with the CDF", he writes, "was making me cry out for more love and more justice in the Church."

He is scathing about the CDF's claim, as voiced by Cardinal Ratzinger in his letter to Cardinal König, that the congregation had simply sent Dupuis "some confidential questions". How so, when in fact their document "began with fierce charges about the orthodoxy of Dupuis' book", and "explicitly accused" him "of directly violating church teaching"? As for the word "dialogue" repeatedly used by Cardinal Ratzinger in his letter, "if this is dialogue, I would hate to see confrontation."

The hearing before the CDF took place on Monday September 4, 2000. On the weekend before, Dupuis received from the CDF a 15-page "Notification" about his book. "I would indeed be a heretic", he told friends, "if I believed what they say I do. But I don't."

With the Notification came the text of a declaration entitled *Dominus Iesus* which was to cause uproar. Dupuis was universally understood to be its chief target. It distinguished between Christian "theological faith" revealed supernaturally from above and the belief of non-Christians merely founded on their human experience. The latter, therefore, were in "a gravely deficient situation." For good measure, the declaration added that Churches without a valid episcopate and Eucharist were not proper Churches at all.

It was very hot in Rome on 4 September. Inside the room, copies of Dupuis' book were strewn across a table. No drink was provided. Cardinal Ratzinger sat in the centre. On his right were Archbishop (later Cardinal) Tarcisio Bertone as CDF secretary and Fr (later Cardinal) Angelo Amato as CDF consultor. On his left were Gerald O'Collins, Dupuis himself and the Jesuit General, Fr Kolvenbach.

The meeting lasted for two hours. Cardinal Ratzinger invited O'Collins, Dupuis' chosen advocate, to make his case. The CDF critics had not liked Dupuis' presentation of Jesus Christ, the Incarnate Word of God, as limited by his human condition. They wanted to say that the revelation of God in him was absolute and final. But Dupuis never used the word "Absolute" except for God the Father, the source of salvation. O'Collins countered that this was orthodox. Dupuis knew the tradition backwards and his exposition was in line with the seminal Council of Chalcedon in 451 about the two natures of Christ.

As for limitation, O'Collins pointed out that the scriptural account of revelation is strongly angled towards the future. It is only then that we shall see face to face; now we see in a glass darkly.

Dupuis' image of God is that of the Potter working with his two hands, the Word and the Spirit. The three are distinct but can never be separated. The Word as such sows seeds of faith before, during and after the coming of the Word Incarnate, while always referring to it. Similarly the Spirit is active and present before, during and after the Incarnation, while always referring to it. Again and again O'Collins repeated: to distinguish is not to separate.

It was clear by the end that the Notification could not proceed.

Part III: Friends

Dupuis reminded Cardinal Ratzinger that he had sent 260 pages in reply to the CDF's charges. Ratzinger looked embarrassed. "You cannot expect us to read and study all that material," he said.

He made one last try. He asked Dupuis: "Would you agree your book could be read in the light of *Dominus Iesus*?" "Eminence, you ask too much of me" was the reply.

A revised, much shorter, version of the Notification reached Dupuis from the CDF on December 6. It no longer accused him of "grave errors". Instead, it spoke of "serious ambiguities". But Dupuis was not asked to change a line of the book. On 16 December he signed.

In view of *The Tablet*'s support, he came to London in October 2001 to deliver the Open Day lecture. He entitled it "Christianity and Other Religions: from confrontation to dialogue," echoing the title of a subsequent volume he had written in which he clarified the relationship between the Church and the other religions as being one of "asymmetrical complementarity." An edited version of the lecture appeared in three instalments ("The storm of the Spirit," October 20; "God is always greater," October 27; "The work of the Potter", November 3). To this day some teachers recommend these *Tablet* articles as the most accessible introduction to Dupuis' thought.

He also went to Vienna in 2003 to thank Cardinal König. On July 16 the two men talked all day. Christa Pongratz-Lippitt recorded part of their conversation for posterity, kept it and later transcribed it. *The Tablet*, judging it too hot to handle on the eve of Easter 2004, published extracts.

Dominus Iesus was "a big step backwards," the two agreed. The CDF, Dupuis recalled, "say that revelation in Jesus Christ is complete, final, definitive and all the rest – but that is *impossible*" (voice rising) "– the New Testament says that God will be fully revealed at the end of time. So how can they say what they say?"

To the end, the CDF persisted in challenging and harassing Dupuis. He had to fight depression, but never had any doubt that he was broadly right. "If we do not go this way," he would tell me, "we shall have no credibility left."

O'Collins always held a trump card, and did not hesitate to use it. He ended a letter to *The Tablet* for December 12, 1998, for example: "to condemn Dupuis' book would, I fear, be to condemn the Pope himself." For in his encyclical *Redemptoris Missio* and elsewhere, John Paul II had insisted that the Spirit's presence and activity extend beyond individuals to "society and history, peoples, cultures and religions."

Dupuis continues to have his supporters and his critics. For myself, I can only say that as one struggles to grasp his vision, vistas suddenly appear as though illuminated by flashes of lightning in the dark to enlarge one's awareness of the Christian Trinitarian mystery at work throughout the world. Never was that assurance more necessary than now.

16
Janette ("Jan") Gray RSM (1952–2016)

Jan Gray's first book, *Neither Escaping Nor Exploiting Sex: Women's Celibacy* (1995), emerged from her Masters in Theology for the Melbourne College of Divinity (now University of Divinity) and became a best-seller. Her supervisors and examiners called for its publication. In it she explored how celibate women live their sexuality and how their personal challenges yield valuable ideas about human relationships and ecological awareness. The book symbolized a lifelong, passionate concern to educate herself and others.

Born in Adelaide, South Australia, Jan received a B.A. and Dip. Ed. from Macquarie University (Sydney) before becoming a Sister of Mercy in January 1976. She taught history at several colleges in South Australia. A contemporary from those years recalls: "she was one of those rare breed of teachers who make a real difference in the lives of students *and their parents*."

A love for theology and spirituality took over, and she received her PhD at the University of Cambridge for a dissertation on "The Christian Anthropology of Marie-Dominique Chenu." She had been a graduate student at Emmanuel College, Cambridge, and supervised by Professor Nicholas Lash. At the time of her death, she was completing a book on this French Dominican who had proved very influential in preparing for the Second Vatican Council: *Theology for Global People*: *Chenu*. During her time of study in Cambridge, she also lectured for the Cambridge Federation of Theological Colleges. Joining with Catholic and other Christian scholars in the work of theological education became a definitive commitment.

Home in Australia, Jan lectured at several academic centres in Perth: Edith Cowan University, Murdoch University, and the University of Notre Dame. The units she taught included introduction to theology, fundamental or foundational theology, Christology or the doctrine of Christ, the Holy Trinity, women in the church, faith and culture, and the theology of the human person. She also specialized in ecclesiology: the human person in the community of the church, "a community she always saw as ecumenically and untidily open" (Brendan Byrne, see below).

Across Australia, Jan was also much in demand for lectures not only to the Sisters of Mercy and other religious associations but also to men and women engaged in education. Her themes ranged from "What Jesus came to say to us: evangelisation for today" and "Leadership in the postmodern world and church" to "Directions in religious life" and "The Catholic School's mission of hope to the world."

Leaving Western Australia, Jan joined the faculty of the Jesuit Theological College in Parkville (Melbourne), and from that base lectured and supervised dissertations at the United Faculty of Theology (2002–14) within the Melbourne College of Divinity (now the University of Divinity). She became Principal of Jesuit

Theological College (2012–14). With the dissolution of the United Faculty of Theology, she began lecturing at the newly established Pilgrim College (Uniting Church of Australia). For years she was book review editor for *Pacifica*, recognized in its day as the leading, ecumenical journal in Australia.

Jan had a passion for life and for all that enriched life: theatre, opera, music, art, literature, history and, above all, theology or thinking, imagining, and talking about God. After her death, tributes poured in from past students. One recalled her as "a learned and lively lecturer." Another, perhaps the most gifted and demanding person she ever taught, wrote: "I remember looking forward to her classes, which effortlessly interwove theology, art, and spirituality." She drew creatively on so many sources to make a point.

Jan often spoke about her father, Roger, to whom she was exceptionally close. From his lifelong involvement in the labour movement, she inherited much of her own passion for social justice.

Jan was always very dedicated to her family, to the Sisters of Mercy, to religious women around Australia, and to her students and academic colleagues. "A stalwart friend to so many in need" was the way one her colleagues described her.

Serious problems with her pancreas meant repeated surgery in the last years of her life. As one former student remarked, "I marvelled at how much of her humour and strength she retained and how much she was able to minister to others, even as each potential Eureka-moment in her treatment soured in turn."

The fact that we had both studied and lived at the University of Cambridge bound us together. We would swop stories about its faculty and others. Her love of theological learning, ecumenical commitment, and sense of life's comedy made it very easy to relate to Jan. She had a flatteringly high opinion of my 2011 *Rethinking Fundamental Theology*,[39] and I hoped to repay her esteem by inviting her to join me in teaching a course. But her illness intervened.

Jan died just as the Year of Mercy proclaimed by Pope Francis came to an end in December 2016. When concluding his homily at her memorial service (January 6, 2017), Brendan Byrne SJ remarked: "we are commemorating today one who, in response to her vocation, placed her multiple talents and energy at the service of mercy, not just for a year but her whole life long. Much though we might wish that her life had been longer, let us be thankful for the gift Jan has been to us all and surrender her gently to the Lord."

Let me now insert with grateful thanks the full text of that homily.

****

The Gospel that I have just read (Matt 20:1-16) would not be one we would often expect to hear at Requiem or Memorial Masses. I've given a lot of thought as to why the Sisters of Mercy would have chosen it to be proclaimed at this Memorial celebration for their beloved sister Jan, whose loss they, and all of us here present, feel so keenly.

The parable told in the Gospel is about workers, day labourers in a vineyard. Jan often spoke about her father, Roger, to whom she was exceptionally close, and who, all his long life, has been involved in the labour movement. She doubtless inherited a good measure of her own passion for social justice from him.

She also inherited something else. Early last year, to add to her

---

[39] Oxford: Oxford University Press, 2011.

serious health problems from which she was slowly recovering, she slipped and fell heavily in her bathroom, breaking several bones. The response from her father, when she called to break the news, was, "There you go—clumsy, as ever." "Well." retorted Jan, "It was from you I inherited it!"

And, at one level, the parable *is* about social justice. To those who had worked all day and who grumbled because the latecomers were being paid as much as they, the vineyard owner pointed out that he was not being unjust; he was paying them the agreed amount. If he chose to pay the same to the latecomers, he was simply crowning justice with generosity and mercy. They too had families to feed and clothe. He was paying them what later social teaching would describe as a "living wage"—a wage that sees human labour, not in purely contractual terms, but as an essential element of life in community, the basis of a society designed for human flourishing rather than simply competition and production.

Like all Jesus' parables, the Workers in the Vineyard projects a distinctive vision of God. Jan was above all a theologian, one whose vocation it was—as the etymology of the word "theologian" suggests—to think and talk about God. What is the image of God that emerges from this parable? We should, of course, be careful about immediately identifying the main character in a parable with God. In this case, though, I think we can.

Like a few other characters in Jesus' parables, the workers who had toiled all day and grumbled project an image of God as One whose assessment of human worth is strictly tied to achievement. None of us could comfortably face such a God, yet so often we find that notion of the divine lurking in the recesses of our imagination and, more widely, in the life of our Church. We have to do a lot of "meriting" according to our new translation of the liturgy!

Over against that inadequate understanding, the parable presents the image of God represented by the owner of the vineyard: the generous, merciful God who is more interested in the well-being of persons and communities than in whatever work we do.

That was certainly the image of God that Vatican II recaptured for the Church, and Jan was nothing if not a passionate promoter of the teaching and spirit of the Council. Her Cambridge doctoral thesis was entitled, *The Christian Anthropology of Marie-Dominique Chenu*, a seminal theologian of Vatican II, mentor in particular of its most influential theological expert, Yves Congar.

We note the word "anthropology" in the title. Jan taught especially the courses on the human person—in sin and in grace, in loss and in hope. She also specialized in ecclesiology: the human person in the community of the Church, a community she always saw as ecumenically and untidily open rather than closed in on itself in smug perfection.

Jan was a splendid teacher. She communicated not just information but theological commitment and passion. Our overseas students in particular loved her. Over the last few days so many have sent messages, recalling her teaching with gratitude, lamenting her loss. One was so discouraged by the difficulty of the early days of his studies that he was on the point of asking to go home. Jan's gentle encouragement persuaded him to stay. He did and is now pursuing graduate studies in the area her teaching opened up for him. She was chuffed that he allowed her to call him by an abbreviation of his name otherwise used strictly within the family circle—though Jan confessed to me that she simply couldn't manage the longer version!

Part III: Friends

Returning, finally, to the parable. Jan was something of a labourer herself. She laboured constantly under ill health. Her body seemed to be a burden for her to carry around. It did not serve well all she wanted to do, so as to meet the countless calls on her teaching and expertise. I think especially of the long flights to Perth and other distant parts. She had so much to give—and give she did, but at what cost we can hardly guess.

Aware of her administrative gifts and the general respect in which she was held, we Jesuits asked her to be Principal of Jesuit Theological College. She most capably and generously filled this leadership role, though by this time her health was seriously in question. Her kindness to Geoff King during the onset of *his* debilitating illness was legendary. The decision of the Jesuit province to wind up JTC as a teaching institution, taken at a time when she was herself too ill to participate in the decision-making, was a bitter disappointment to her—as it was to many. However, she never allowed her disappointment to blunt the professional edge of her leadership of the college to the end.

Ultimately, Jan was not to be among those who laboured the whole day long. Her life was cut short when, as one of Australia's leading theologians, she still had so much to give. These are mysteries we can only leave to God.

We heard just the briefest snatch of Paul's teaching on the resurrection in the First Reading (1 Cor 15:51-52). As Jan herself pointed out in the reflection read by Sr Helen, with regard to our human, bodily life, Paul speaks of change and transformation. As a systematic theologian, Jan rested her theology on a firm biblical base. What she wrote shows that she had pondered those words and the hope they express very deeply and very often. Our Christian faith, leads us to believe that what she pondered in hope she now enjoys in reality and sight.

As Bishop Greg O'Kelly, SJ, pointed out to me just a couple of days ago, Jan died just as Pope Francis's Year of Mercy came to a close. We are commemorating today one who, in response to her vocation, placed her multiple talents and energy at the service of mercy, not just for a year but her whole life long. Much though we might wish that her life had been longer, let us be thankful for the gift Jan has been to us all and surrender her gently to the Lord.

17
Peter-Hans Kolvenbach SJ (1926–2016)

On the afternoon of September 13, 1983, a few hours after he was elected the 29th Superior General of the Society of Jesus, Peter-Hans Kolvenbach slipped out of the Jesuit headquarters in Rome to take a walk. An Italian lady saw him leaving the building and asked: "Are you attending the general congregation of the Jesuits?" "Yes," he told her. "Well," she said, "I wouldn't have voted for Father Kolvenbach." "Let me assure you," he replied, "I didn't." She had expected the election of the Italian Fr Joseph Pittau, and obviously had no idea with whom she was speaking.

Born in Holland on November 30, 1928, Fr Kolvenbach entered the Society of Jesus in September 1948. After studies in Nijmegen (Holland) and Beirut (Lebanon), in 1961 he was ordained a priest in the rite of the Armenian Catholic Church. He had the Dutch gift for languages. He not only spoke European and Middle-Eastern languages, but was also a specialist in linguistics. He spent years teaching linguistics in Beirut, as well as in Paris and the Hague. During the civil war in Lebanon, a stray rocket hit his room in the Jesuit residence in Beirut and destroyed everything, including his books and papers. Later, when he became superior general of the Jesuit order, his companions in Rome noticed how he kept his room more or less empty, and went to the library to look up books and journals.

Two years after coming to Rome in 1981 to serve as rector of the Pontifical Oriental Institute, he attended the 33rd General Congregation and was elected superior general at the first ballot. The Jesuits needed a leader endowed with his undemonstrative holiness and a practical wisdom honed by international and wartime experience.

Fr Pedro Arrupe, the predecessor of Fr Kolvenbach, had suffered a major stroke at Rome's airport on August 7, 1981, after returning from an exhausting visit to the Philippines and Thailand. Elected superior general in 1965, Fr Arrupe gave himself unstintingly to his work as a charismatic spiritual leader within the Society of Jesus and beyond. As his health began to decline, he raised with Pope John Paul II the question of resignation but was told to continue. Now that he was immobilized, the Pope set aside the constitutions of the Society of Jesus and appointed his personal delegate, Fr (later Cardinal) Paolo Dezza (assisted by Fr Pittau who was summoned from Japan), to run the Society of Jesus. Fr Dezza did his wise best to secure as soon as possible the papal approval for a general congregation, at which Jesuits from around the world could elect a successor to Fr Arrupe.

They were difficult years from late 1981 until normal Jesuit government resumed with John Paul II allowing the general congregation to meet in September 1983. Dezza was the personification of kindness and encouragement during that time. Distinguished for his great wisdom and power as an orator, he had been for years the confessor to Pope Paul VI and to Pope John Paul

I during the brief month of his pontificate. He was delighted when he could step down and pass leadership on to a normally elected superior general.

John Paul II related more easily with Fr Kolvenbach than he had with Fr Arrupe; it seemed a matter of better "body chemistry." On key issues and priorities the policies of Arrupe and Kolvenbach seemed indistinguishable. In an interview with the magazine *Choisir* (July/August 2006), Fr Kolvenbach said: "Faith and justice are not parallel actions; they go together, because both are inspired by the same charity. Justice without charity is injustice, and faith without charity is a faith without effect." These could have been words from Fr Arrupe.

Fr Kolvenbach went on to lead the Society of Jesus for twenty-five years. As an Armenian priest, he was the first Jesuit general who belonged to an Eastern rite (rather than the Latin rite) of the Catholic Church. Eventually, with the permission of Pope Benedict XVI, he offered his resignation. In January 2008 it was accepted by the 35th General Congregation, which elected as successor to Fr Kolvenbach, Fr Adolfo Nicolás, a Spaniard who had spent his active Jesuit life in Japan and the Philippines. As soon as he could do so, Fr Kolvenbach returned to his beloved Lebanon, and died in Beirut on November 26, 2016.

During twenty-two of Fr Kolvenbach's years as superior general, I lived across Rome at the Gregorian University. I came to appreciate more and more his quiet sanctity, holy prudence, high intelligence, and, one must add, brilliant sense of humour. He stood tall when faced with the persecution of his fellow Jesuits.

When a military death squad in El Salvador murdered six Jesuits, with their housekeeper and her daughter, one night in November

1989, many Catholics expected that John Paul II would have personally celebrated a requiem Mass for the dead in St Peter's Basilica, or at least have asked a senior cardinal to do so on his behalf. But no such papal gesture was forthcoming. A huge crowd jammed into the Church of the Gesù for a Mass celebrated with extraordinary intensity and presided over by Fr Kolvenbach. After the service an American priest remarked to me: "If the Polish military had dragged six priests out of bed and shot them in their garden, we would be hearing about it from the Pope for weeks. But those six priests in El Salvador made the mistake of endorsing and practising liberation theology."

After I arrived to teach full time at the Gregorian, I came to know a Vietnamese Jesuit, Joseph Nguyen who was studying across the street at the Pontifical Biblical Institute. As the war was drawing to a close in Vietnam, he took early examinations and hurried home to experience the surrender of Saigon and then years of work in a prison camp. When he left Rome in 1975, Fr Arrupe, still very much the Jesuit superior general, went out to the airport to see him off. Joseph returned twenty years later as the Jesuit provincial of Vietnam and a delegate to our 34th general congregation (1995), a meeting which drew representatives from Jesuit provinces around the world to update our law and redefine our priorities for the years to come. I can still hear the quiet voice of my Vietnamese friend Joseph, when he told me the story of his twenty years away from Rome and the incredible joy he felt on arrival at the Roman airport to be welcomed personally by Fr Kolvenbach.

On a personal level, I remain intensely grateful for the unwavering support he gave to Fr Jacques Dupuis, my older companion at the Gregorian who, from 1998 was investigated by the Congregation for the Doctrine of the Faith. Eventually, the CDF issued a "notification" that, without asking for any changes in the text, declared that (unspecified) passages in Dupuis's *Toward a Christian Theology of Religious Pluralism* could lead people astray. On the one occasion when Dupuis met Cardinal Joseph Ratzinger and other members of the CDF, Fr Kolvenbach spoke up firmly. Serious accusations had been made against Dupuis's book, but no specific passages were cited to illustrate the alleged errors.

Years before Cardinal Ratzinger also brought Fr Kolvenbach and me together over *The Ratzinger Report*[40], a book in which the Cardinal expressed his views on a wide range of topics. In the summer of 1985, when I had just been elected dean of the Gregorian's theology faculty and made a brief stopover in New York, the director of a fundraising operation, the Gregorian Foundation, took the occasion of my visit to arrange a press conference—in the spirit of "come and meet the new dean." Inevitably Ratzinger's book came up in the question period. The fact that I took my distance from it was widely reported. I had made it clear that Ratzinger's point of view often differed substantially from that of John Paul II's and that the book had saddened many people in Rome.

On my return to Rome at the start of September, I found a letter waiting for me from Fr Kolvenbach. He told me that he had received a number of complaints from bishops and other church officials about what I had said in New York. But by that time the Pope himself had publicly distanced himself from *The Ratzinger Report*. Speaking to journalists during a journey to Africa in the first half of August, John Paul II had commented: "what Cardinal Ratzinger said is his own opinion (*parere suo*)," and added: "He is free to express his opinion." The Pope had made it quite clear that

---
[40] San Francisco: Ignatius Press, 1985.

he did not share the Cardinal's decidedly one-sided and negative assessment of Catholic life in the aftermath of the Second Vatican Council. The Pope's remarks defused the situation for me. Over lunch with Fr Kolvenbach I undertook to be more discreet, noted that the Holy Father's comments had come at the right time, and added: "I do agree with the old adage *quod licet Iovi non licet bovi* (what's ok for Jupiter is not ok for an ox)." The Pope could express his mind publicly but that didn't mean that I could.

Fr Kolvenbach died on the feast of a young Jesuit seminarian St John Berchmans, who also came from the Netherlands. The holiness of Berchmans has often been characterized as that of "a cheerful giver." Fr Kolvenbach lived four times as long as the young saint. But, right to the end, he remained like Berchmans "a cheerful giver."

The loveliest tribute to Fr Kolvenbach came from our present superior general, Fr Arturo Sosa, SJ, who, at an evening Mass in the Church of the Gesù (December 2, 2016), used images from Kolvenbach's beloved Lebanon: "We all have many memories of Fr Kolvenbach. We could spend the whole night recalling moments alongside him. To remember Fr Kolvenbach is to remember a companion of Jesus, a close brother, a priest who reinvigorated life in us, a believer full of hope engaged in the proclamation of the gospel and in building peace, a just man. Therefore, as we did at the beginning of the Eucharist, we can say with the Psalmist: 'The righteous man will flourish like the palm tree; he will grow like a cedar in Lebanon. Planted in the house of the Lord, he will flourish in the courts of our God.'"

18
Cardinal Carlo Maria Martini, SJ (1927–2012)

Many Vatican observers believed that, had Pope John Paul II died in the 1990s and not lived and remained in office until 2005, Cardinal Carlo Martini might well have succeeded him. Even after Martini developed Parkinson's disease, a sizeable block of cardinals voted for him at the first ballot in the conclave that began on the afternoon of April 18, 2005. But he is reported to have drawn their attention to his physical condition, clearing the way for Cardinal Joseph Ratzinger to be elected the following day and take the name of Benedict XVI.

Martini will be remembered as an outstanding Archbishop of Milan (1980–2002), a leader in encouraging believers to become true Christians, a major contributor in providing the most accurate text of the Greek New Testament, and a revered rector of two major Jesuit institutions in Rome: the Pontifical Biblical Institute (1969–78) and the Pontifical Gregorian University (1978–79).

Martini's life took a new turn in December 1979 when he

was appointed Archbishop of Milan, one of the largest and most prominent dioceses in the Catholic world. He constantly supported a wider role for the ministry of women, social justice—especially for immigrants, refugees, and other suffering minorities—more qualified positions in matters of human sexuality and the right to be allowed to die, and more collegiality or shared decision-making at every level in the Church.

Famously he reached out to young people through monthly meditative meetings (based on the Scriptures) in the Milan cathedral. He contacted the young who did not attend by writing a welcoming letter to them and then asking those present to take a copy for one of their friends who was disengaged from the Church.

Martini lived and breathed the teaching of the Second Vatican Council (1962-65). He was always open to relations with Jews, other Christians, those of other faiths, and those who professed no religious faith at all.

The press cherished Martini, not least the Milan daily, *Corriere della Sera*. That paper carried a remarkable exchange of letters between him and Professor Umberto Eco on ecological, political, social, and religious challenges to the Church and the world. This exchange was eventually published as *Belief or Nonbelief: A Confrontation*.[41]

When Martini went to Milan, the "anni di piombo (years of lead)" still continued, with terrorist organizations killing hundreds of people. In May 1980, after the Red Brigade assassinated a young journalist, Walter Tobagi, in revenge for what he had written about them, Martini took the service. He spoke of a "mystery of meaninglessness and madness." He also reminded the congregation

---

[41] New York: Arcade Publishing, 2000.

of that great certainty to be found in the Bible: "What is meaningless can gain a meaning." The prayers of the faithful which followed this homily showed most movingly how Martini had helped those in terrible sorrow to see and affirm meaning. Stella Tobagi, now widowed with two small children, sat with her arms around them, while her sister read her prayer: "Lord, we pray for those who killed Walter, and for all people who think that violence is the only right way for resolving problems. May the power of your Spirit change the hearts of men, and out of Walter's death may there be born a hope which the force of arms will never be able to defeat."

The son of an engineer, Martini was born in Turin (just two months before Joseph Ratzinger), attended a Jesuit high school, and in September 1944 entered a Jesuit novitiate. He studied philosophy and theology at two centers in northern Italy and was ordained a priest in July 1952—his ordination at age twenty-five was and remains remarkably young for a Jesuit.

In 1958, Martini was awarded a doctorate (summa cum laude) at the Gregorian University for a dissertation on historical aspects of the resurrection of Jesus. After teaching for several years at Chieri, a theological faculty in northern Italy, he received a second doctorate (also summa cum laude) at the Biblical Institute for a thesis on questions about the text of Luke's Gospel in the light of two ancient "authorities," the fourth-century *Codex Vaticanus* and the *Bodmer Papyrus XIV* from the early third century.

From 1962, he held a chair in textual criticism at the Biblical Institute. From the 1960s, he was the only Catholic in an elite team of scholars headed by Professor Kurt Aland at the Institute for New Testament Research at the University of Münster in Germany. They produced the first edition of *The Greek New Testament* in 1966, and

Martini was still on the team when the fourth edition appeared in 1993.

Martini was known as an outstanding director of spiritual "retreats," drawing on the *Spiritual Exercises* of St Ignatius Loyola and subtly applying Ignatian insights by introducing such biblical figures as Abraham, Job, and Moses. Many of those addresses were later published—for instance, four volumes of retreats in the light of Matthew, Mark, Luke, and John.

In 1978 Pope Paul VI invited Martini to preach the annual retreat offered at the Vatican for papal collaborators. A few months later, on July 31, 1978, the Pope signed a document appointing Martini "rector magnificus" of the Gregorian University—apparently the last official act of the Pope, who died on August 6.

After his move to Milan, without neglecting the Archdiocese, Martini accepted invitations to visit Africa, India, Japan, the USA, and other countries. In 1997 he was among a team of cardinals to preach at Westminster Cathedral in London, for the centenary of its foundation. In its spiritual and biblical brilliance, his sermon stood out. Those who heard him speak on that occasion knew that the Catholic Church had lost a pope who would have ranked with the very greatest papal preachers, like St Leo the Great and St Gregory the Great.

I did not hear Martini preaching in Westminster Cathedral, but was with him on another occasion. It was a magic Sunday at Canterbury, to which he came as a guest of Archbishop George Carey. Martini preached in the cathedral, and everything was done with Anglican precision and style. Lunch was a delightful family affair, prepared by the Careys' daughter Rachel and her husband Andy.

Martini also shone on his visit to Australia in 1996. In Sydney at a lunch for one thousand business leaders chaired by the future Prime Minister, Malcolm Turnbull, he encouraged better ethical practices. At a meeting in St Mary's Church, West Melbourne, his audience included the retiring archbishop Sir Frank Little and his successor, Archbishop (later Cardinal) George Pell. Addressing them, Martini remarked that with his vision and hospitality Little reminded him of Abraham. Then he told Pell: "You remind me of Moses, a leader and the meekest of men. I wish for you the gift of meekness."

A tall, aristocratic figure, Martini spoke with gentle and measured authority. On official occasions he had to dress in the full regalia of a cardinal, but preferred to wear simple, clerical dress.

He took his distance from *Dominus Iesus*, a document produced by Cardinal Ratzinger's office in 2000. Among other questionable features, the document characterized many Christian communities as not being "proper churches." Martini called *Dominus Iesus* "theologically rather dense, peppered with quotations, and not easy to read."

After he retired at the age of seventy-five, Martini spent as much time as he could in Jerusalem, the city that mattered most to him in the world.

One way or another I frequently met Martini during the 1970s. In 1977, he was a genial host when I attended the dinner for his fiftieth birthday given at the Biblical Institute where he was still rector. I marvelled at the kind but firm way he "shut down" a garrulous, old cardinal whose long speech about his experiences in Rome had barely reached 1930.

Two years later, now as rector at the Gregorian, Martini welcomed Pope John Paul II to the university and gracefully guided proceedings through the morning and over lunch with the community. Looking at Martini shepherding the Pope around with the ease of a born leader, I thought: "You are finished now at the Gregorian." Within weeks he was appointed Archbishop of Milan, and we lost a rector whose life persistently drew its inspiration and strength from daily contact with the Bible.

For the requiem in Milan when Cardinal Martini died in 2012, Pope Benedict sent a message which quoted a prayer from a homily preached by Martini on March 29, 1980. The prayer expresses intensely his radically biblical spirituality: "We ask you, Lord, to turn us into spring water for others, broken bread for our brothers and sisters, light for those walking through the darkness, life for those who grope in death's shadows. Lord, be the life of the world. Lord, guide us toward your Easter; together we will walk toward you; we will carry your cross; we will experience communion with your resurrection. We will walk toward the heavenly Jerusalem, toward the Father, alongside you."

19
Eugene ("Gene") (1934–2010) and Maureen McCarthy (1936–1999)

Dr Eugene ("Gene") McCarthy, who died in New York on September 16, 2010, and his wife Maureen, who passed away on September 3, 1999, attracted attention wherever they went in life. Gene was always a tall, handsome presence. Maureen's bright red hair framed her green eyes that sparkled with delight over the people she met. This couple showed me and many others how Jesus and the Holy Spirit can work in married life.

A Trappist priest, for years their spiritual adviser, once remarked to them: "Every marriage has trials, and progression through those trials is the seedbed for growth in durability and love within the marriage." Three painful crises proved the truth of this observation.

Two Painful Crises

Married in 1958 and now with three teenage boys, Gene and Maureen faced their first painful test in the late 1970s. Maureen had become increasingly dependent upon alcohol and this put the marriage at risk. But she entered an Alcoholics Anonymous program and went on to assist many others on their path to sobriety. She turned into what Gene called the "den mother" for AA members on the Upper East Side of New York. Increasingly aware of the sacramental grace of their married vocation, Gene acknowledged his own part in causing her disease through his extremely busy life as a professor of public health at Cornell University.

When their eldest son Joe, a gentle and lovable giant, was a sophomore at St John's College, Queens, in 1980/81, he became involved with a drug crowd and this triggered the onset of paranoid schizophrenia. "Maureen and I," Gene recalled, "now had a son suffering from a mental illness that was to prove fatal." But, "thanks to the sacrament of our marriage, this experience united us even more as one in Christ."

Joe was in and out of hospital, joined AA, related well to other members, spent a final Thanksgiving with his parents in 1984, and died the following Saturday. He had found some liquor, started to drink again, and died when he aspirated some of his own vomit into his lungs. The death of Gene's and Maureen's first born followed quickly on the heels of her own struggle with alcoholism. A third crisis came much later.

Fruitful Years (1984–1996)

After Joe's death, Gene and Maureen both took time out

to make twenty-day retreats and considered the possibility of going into monastic life, Gene into the Trappists and Maureen into the Trappistines. But a Trappist priest, who had trained as a psychoanalyst under Carl Gustav Jung, rocked back and forth in his chair as he listened to the proposal and finally said: "Gene, you're married. That's all I have to say. You're married." On another occasion Gene asked the same old friend about St Teresa of Avila and her "spiritual rooms" in *The Interior Castle*. He wanted to know what room he was in, and was told: "You're only just across the drawbridge, McCarthy!"

More realistic now about the future direction of their lives and responsibilities toward their sons John and Paul, Gene and Maureen took to reciting the Divine Office and did that together, if possible. "You and I are a community," Maureen often said. They also attended daily Mass, either together or separately, according to their schedules. They continued to draw much strength from an annual retreat made during Holy Week, and started going each year to the shrine of Our Lady in Lourdes in the South of France.

On their first visit to Lourdes, they continued on to Rome and came by my office at the Gregorian University. They were checking effective ways for helping those who studied and taught at Church-affiliated institutions in the eternal city. That was the first time we met, and I was at once impressed by their matter-of-fact approach to finding out what they might support financially and personally.

At the Gregorian we already had the practice of enriching our programs for graduate students in theology by securing visiting professors who offered courses for six weeks or even a whole semester. But it was a somewhat hand-to-mouth affair, which depended on juggling available funds within a tight budget. Thanks to the McCarthy Family Foundation, we could now issue regular invitations on a firm basis.

Gene proposed that these visiting stars should also deliver a public lecture, which was to be published in our quarterly, the *Gregorianum*. One of the most memorable of these McCarthy Lectures was delivered by Bishop Eduard Lohse, a New Testament scholar and retired Lutheran bishop. He presented very positively what we can glean from the New Testament about St Paul's view of the ministry of St Peter. In the front row of the huge audience, Gene and Maureen sat alongside Cardinal Joseph Ratzinger. In April 2005 he was to be elected Pope and succeed to the chair of St Peter.

Each year Maureen asked a Trappistine friend to prepare a beautiful scroll to be presented to the current McCarthy Professor. Written by hand in blue and gold, these were the most beautiful academic parchments I have ever seen. Before each of the public lectures, Maureen prepared a large display of flowers to decorate the podium. After the lecture and discussion ended, she would come forward to speak and present the scroll. For the dinner that followed she looked after the seating arrangements with the eye of a practised hostess.

The visits to Rome allowed Gene and Maureen to meet another remarkable couple, Prince Frank and Princess Orietta Pogson Doria Pamphilj, whose palace was only a very short walk from the Gregorian. On one unforgettable Sunday evening, when their chef was enjoying his regular day off, Orietta insisted on cooking a meal for Gene, Maureen, Frank, and myself. She made Gene and me sit down with Frank, while she and Maureen served. At that stage Maureen already had one major operation for cancer behind her, while Orietta was suffering from a slow-moving, malignant disease. Between courses, the two ladies limped around the table in the wonderful dining room of the Palazzo Doria. It was embarrassing for Gene and myself not to be allowed to get up and do the serving. But the Princess Orietta and Maureen insisted!

Gene and Maureen encouraged and financially supported me and various colleagues in setting up four international conferences (we called them "Summits") which were held at St Joseph's Seminary, Yonkers, just after Easter 1996, 1998, 2000, and 2003. These meetings drew together specialists from various disciplines and Christian denominations to present papers on central themes: Christ's resurrection (1996), the Trinity (1998), the incarnation (2000), and redemption (2003). In each case the proceedings were published by Oxford University Press.

On the occasion of the first "summit," Kenneth Woodward wrote a cover story on the resurrection of *Newsweek*. That issue not only sold exceptionally well but also encouraged the press and television networks to cover our meeting. ABC, CNN, and NBC could not have done more for us.

From the time we first met, I gradually learned more about the earlier life of Gene and Maureen: her studies at Lesley College (Boston), and his studies at Boston College (where he was the valedictorian for his class). at Yale Medical School, and at Johns Hopkins (for a Master's in public health). They were on the road campaigning when John Kennedy ran for president. Later Gene was to work as a health adviser to Senator Robert Kennedy in implementing Medicare and Medicaid, and Maureen enjoyed a warm friendship with Ethel Kennedy.

In 1961 they flew down to Asunción, Paraguay. With her mastery of Spanish, Maureen flourished during their three years in Latin

America. Appointed by USAID as a public health adviser, Gene was responsible for programs in rural towns and villages. They both worked effectively to reduce the incidence of tuberculosis. Maureen received a gold medal from the Paraguay School of Nursing and Midwifery in recognition of her work.

They went home to the USA in late 1964 and Gene took up an appointment with the School of Public Health at Columbia University and then with the Department of Public Health at Cornell Medical School (also in New York). Gene left an enduring mark through his research and advocacy of the health benefits of "the second opinion." He persuaded both health insurers and pension and welfare associations of the need to have an opinion from a second doctor before undergoing elective surgery and other major medical treatment. Many groups made that requirement mandatory.

Over the years I became more and more aware of the wide range of institutions and individuals that Gene and Maureen quietly supported, both personally and financially. Their spiritual networking included many diocesan priests and bishops, Benedictines, Carmelites, Jesuits, Passionists, Trappists, Trappistines, and others.

An intellectual who also knew how to act in very effective ways, Gene was less skilled with words than Maureen. She published two volumes of fresh, lyrical poems about human and divine love: *Catching the Spirit: Songs of Light and Shadow* (1994) and *Prelude to Passion: Journey of Love* (1999). A painter as well as a poet, she became an unofficial spiritual director to many. She had great ease in talking about divine and human affairs with a full range of people, including those in the priesthood and religious life. They drew much from her affectionate support, palpable love of Jesus, and willingness to be led by the Holy Spirit.

Third and Final Trial

Gene and Maureen plunged into their third and final trial in September 1996. An operation on Maureen's knee revealed a synovial sarcoma. Over the next three years the cancer spread and she faced repeated surgery and chemotherapy programs. She constantly drew strength from the Eucharist, *lectio divina* (or meditative reading of the Scriptures), ministering to other patients, especially the terminally ill, and contacts with friends and family—in particular, her two grandchildren. She learned centring prayer from Abbot Thomas Keating, and turned constantly to the Lord: "Be my food for my passage through death, O good and loving Jesus." When others anxiously asked her about her physical and emotional travail, she would say simply: "Jesus carries me."

Gene became her "100 per cent caregiver," as he put it. One could see them growing closer and closer in that fierce challenge of her final illness. A profound spiritual peace flowed from them. They communicated to others so much love and compassion.

During their lifetime Gene and Maureen sometimes teased each other in religious terms. He would call her "Mother Superior," and she would address him as "My Abbot." Behind this jesting, a tried and tested spirituality, in which they ministered to each other the sacrament of matrimony, made them true contemplatives in action. Like many others, I was deeply blessed to have known them.

20
Peter Daniel Steele, SJ (1939–2012)

"Publishing a poem," Peter Steele once said to me, "is like dropping a feather down the Grand Canyon and waiting for the echo." Yet, right to the end of his life, he never stopped delighting in words and sharing his poetry with friends and with anyone who, like him, relished the possibilities of language and rejoiced in the mysterious features of our world.

Born a week before the Second World War began, Peter grew up in Perth, Western Australia, the eldest in a family of three boys. His father had emigrated to Australia from England at the age of nineteen, and became a Catholic (and a serious one) when he married Peter's mother, an Australian of mixed English and Irish stock. A pious boy, Peter grew up intending to become a priest. From his early teens he showed himself, as he put it, "bookish. As Marxists have wrath and kangaroos have grasslands, I had books. Few of them were at home, but the school library was generous in scale, and for years my Christmas present was a subscription to the Central Catholic Library." What he called "Logophilia," a "respectable form of gluttony, gorging on the printed word, took hold of me very early."

Peter was educated by the Christian Brothers, one of whom encouraged Peter to think of joining the Jesuits. He learned something about them and later recalled: "What struck me was the sense that Jesuits knew what they were about. They seemed to be informed, intelligent, and dedicated, and they seemed to want to be useful on a generous scale." Peter could have been talking about himself and the ideals that were to guide his own life.

In January 1957 Peter took two days and three nights to travel by train from Perth to Melbourne to join the Society of Jesus, of which he remained a member until death. From studying at the University of Melbourne and completing his PhD thesis, he moved smoothly to making this campus a base for a lifetime of teaching and writing. In 1993 he was named to a personal chair in English. After retirement in 2005, he became Emeritus Professor and Hon. Professorial Fellow in 2006, and was awarded an honorary doctorate (DLitt) in 2008. Further honorary doctorates came from Notre Dame University (2010) and Australian Catholic University (2011).

The campus of the University of Melbourne and his residence at Newman College were his "local habitation," to borrow the title of a collection of poems and sermons he published in 2010: *A Local Habitation*: *Poems and Homilies*. Generations of students flocked to the lectures and seminars of this soft-spoken priest. They learnt from his wise humanity, his loving eye for detail, and his unfailingly sharp imagination that found so much to approve and rejoice in.

Peter published major works on the Irish satirist and Anglican cleric Jonathan Swift: first, *An Air of Truth Apparent: A Study of Gulliver's Travels* (1968), and then a longer book with the Clarendon Press, *Jonathan Swift: Preacher and Jester* (1978). He also wrote studies of contemporary poets, both Australians and others, *Expatriates: Reflections on Modern Poetry* (1985) and *Peter Porter* (1992), as well as a short study of Samuel Johnson and Dante Alighieri, *Flights of the Mind: Johnson and Dante* (1997).

A fellow of the Australian Academy of the Humanities, Peter held visiting chairs at Georgetown University (Washington, DC), the University of Alberta (Canada), and Loyola University in Chicago. He delivered the Martin D'Arcy Lectures at the University of Oxford, and later published them as *The Autobiographical Passion: Studies in the Self on Show* (1989).

Peter wrote two illustrated books of poems inspired by works of art: *Plenty: Art into Poetry* (2003) and *The Whispering Gallery: Art into Poetry* (2006). Patrick McCaughey, a former Director of the National Gallery of Victoria, wrote an introduction to the first volume, and Gerard Vaughan, also a Director of the National Gallery of Victoria, wrote a foreword to the second.

Peter published other volumes of poetry: *Words from Lilliput* (1973); *Marching on Paradise* (1984); *Invisible Riders* (1999); *The Gossip and the Wine* (2010). *White Knight with Bee-Box*: *New and Selected Poems*, which appeared in 2008, was awarded the Philip Hodgins Medal for poetry in that year. In April 2011 he received the Christopher Brennan Award, given by the Fellowship of Writers for "Lifetime Achievement in Poetry."

From 1985 to 1990, Peter was provincial superior of the Australian Jesuits. When he finished that term of office, he recalled: "the Irish joke, that when a man becomes a bishop he will never again eat a bad meal or be told the truth, is exactly reversed when it comes to being a provincial. He eats, on his peregrinations, a lot of very strange food, and he is told more truth than he can easily deal with." As for the peregrinations, "my predecessor told me that he had travelled half a million miles in his six years' stint, and I would have done all of that, within Australia and beyond it."

For many years Peter preached the Sunday homily, whether at Newman College within the University of Melbourne, at Georgetown University, or wherever else he found himself in the world. Meticulously crafted, these homilies offered a feast of insight, tackling universal questions and issues. They introduce an extraordinary range of subjects: from Robert Bolt's *A Man for All Seasons* to Shakespeare's *Richard II*, from the story of the Prodigal Son to the image of Neil Armstrong stepping onto the moon, from a travel agency named *Please Go Away* to reflections on the nature of heaven. Peter published 86 of these homilies in *Bread for the Journey* (2002).

Diagnosed with liver cancer in late 2006, Peter faced operations, chemotherapy, and blood transfusions with gentle courage, realism, and never a touch of self-pity. A final book, a collection of poems and essays entitled *Braiding the Voices: Essays in Poetry*, was launched at Newman College on June 12, 2012, the day after Peter was awarded an AM (Member in the General Division of the Order of Australia) in the Queen's Birthday Honours. In a wheel chair he was present at the launch to receive long and repeated applause from a large crowd, but could speak very little. A friend of 45 years and himself a notable poet, Professor Christopher Wallace-Crabbe, read two of the poems from the new collection. Peter died quietly fifteen days later in Caritas Christi Hospice (Kew), with his only surviving brother at his bedside.

Part III: Friends

Peter was cherished and loved by his family, students, fellow Jesuits, academic colleagues, and fellow poets—not least by the Nobel laureate Seamus Heaney. Since he was born in the same year but a few months before Peter, Heaney called him "young Steele." As poet, priest, and preacher, Peter Steele touched the lives of those who met him in academic settings and beyond. He never failed in his affable concern for others, insatiable curiosity about all things human and divine, and restless delight in words.

******

"THE ELOQUENCE OF GOD,"

HOMILY PREACHED BY BRENDAN BYRNE AT THE REQUIEM FOR PETER STEELE, SJ. NEWMAN COLLEGE, NEWMAN COLLEGE,

JULY 2, 2012.

Preaching here in this chapel some weeks ago, Peter Steele alluded to the text I have just read, the beginning of the Gospel according to St John, and remarked: "It is profoundly mysterious of course, and the mystery begins with that expression, 'the Word.' We might say that Christ is part of the eloquence of God."

The "eloquence of God": what a wonderful phrase, coined by Peter, to bring fresh life to an ancient article of faith! And how appropriate to recall it now when we are gathered here to celebrate his requiem—Peter, who was so constantly here in this Chapel eloquent about God. And eloquent, not only about God, but about so many other aspects of life, chiefly literary and artistic, in the wider context of this College and this University.

It will fall to others more qualified than I to pay tribute to Peter's achievements as scholar, teacher and poet. Many such tributes have already begun to come in. In this Requiem homily I shall speak of Peter as friend, Jesuit and priest, eloquent about God.

The first sight of Peter, over fifty five years ago, was not, as I recollect, all that promising of friendship to come. He had arrived at the novitiate early on the day appointed for entry after the long train journey from Perth. The rest of us had put off our arrival until the last moment, leaving Peter to a wearisome wait for companionship the whole day long. He had then, and—I think even his close friends would agree—retained throughout his life a capacity to give a fixed look, the kind of look that a sergeant major would have found very useful on parade. It took some time for us, equally though less eloquently confused about it all, to grasp what a remarkable and lovable companion had come to us from Perth.

> In the beginning was the Word. And the Word became flesh and pitched
>
> his tent among us, and we saw his glory, full of grace and truth' (John 1:1, 14).

In the second-last conversation I had with Peter, we agreed that this text should be the Gospel for his Requiem. In the halting words of our last conversation, he reiterated that it was very much the right choice. There is a sense, I'm sure, in which every poem that Peter wrote was an instance of the Word becoming flesh. Our Irish novice master, Ned Riordan, whom Peter loved and admired as much for his wit and intelligence as for his holiness, once made a throw-away remark that greatly intrigued him: "Where most people look out a window and see a cow, a saint sees a creature." Peter looked

out at the world and acquired from his voracious reading an incredible knowledge of anecdotes and facts—quaint, technical, arcane—most

Part III: Friends

of them remote from anything overtly religious or theological, and found in them a spark of the divine glory.

In his early days I sensed in him a certain reserve regarding the Jesuit poet Gerard Manley Hopkins—a reserve towards a figure against whom he might be too readily measured. But some lines from *Pied Beauty* give perfect expression to what drew Peter into the particularity of God's creation:

> Landscape plotted and piece – fold, fallow, and plough;
> And áll trades, their gear and tackle and trim.
> All things counter, original, spare, strange;
> Whatever is fickle, freckled (who knows how?)
> With swift, slow; sweet, sour; adazzle, dim;
> He fathers-forth whose beauty is past change: Praise him.

Peter was very much the Scholar described by the sage Ben Sirach in the 1st Reading:

> (who) seeks out the wisdom of the ancients,
> preserves the sayings of the famous
> penetrates the subtleties of riddles,
> seeks out the hidden meanings of proverbs
> and is at home with the obscurities of parables.
> (Who) sets his heart to rise early
> to seek the Lord who made him,
> who opens his mouth in prayer
> and asks pardon for his sins.

Peter, who was never a good sleeper, certainly set his heart to rise early. And it was as an early riser that he would meet those other early risers and workers: the janitors, porters, and cleaners of the buildings where he worked. And he greeted them not as a busy academic rushing past on his way to higher things, but as a fellow human being, going to his labour as they were busy about theirs. The unfailing courtesy, the witty and cheering word that won their respect and affection flowed from his profound humility, his sense of being thrown into the mix of humanity and standing in as much need of God's grace and succour as anyone—he, who had so little to be modest about.

If he was much loved, as well as respected as Provincial, it was because he met everyone on this simple human level. No one in the Province, no matter how far below him in education, ever felt the weight of his words or put down by his learning. What a blessing for us to have a Provincial who could sit alongside us in our humanity and use his great intelligence, wisdom and articulacy, simply to help us name and so render more manageable our hopes, our fears, our sorrows and our aspirations.

A man fearlessly immersed in the university world and the contest of ideas, Peter never ceased to point and provoke us to be similarly outward-looking to the world. He often appealed to another Johannine text, "God so loved the world ..." (3:16), and stressed that the world which God so loved—and gave his Son for its life—was not some sanitized or past world but the present world in all its squalor, violence and meanness, as well as its beauty, decency and love.

Peter was ordained a priest in Perth on December 12, 1970, the same day as five others of us were ordained here in Melbourne. In preparation for that event we had been sent off to the Carmelite Sisters at Kew to be measured for albs according to our various bodily proportions. No less than 41 years later when concelebrating

Part III: Friends

with Peter a Mass for the Golden Jubilee of his devoted friend Sr Margaret Manion and my own Loreto Sister, Anne, I was startled to see Peter putting on exactly the same alb. Alas, it was not the garment that once it was, nor by now was Peter the slim ordinand that once he was; the strain upon zips and stitches all too clearly showing a growth in stature as well as wisdom before the Lord. But the fact that Peter still wore that alb—besides being a tribute to the needlework of those good sisters many years before—said something about the kind of priest he felt he had been ordained to be.

The 'cultic', the 'celebratory' aspect of the Mass—not so much stressed in post-Vatican II years—was central for him: the proclaimed transformation of bread and wine, the handling of the sacred vessels, the gestures and movement of the Mass as "dance." Last year in his memorable Radio National *Encounter* interview with Margaret Coffey, Peter said that what priesthood has in common with poetry is that each of them has to do with celebration. He went on:

> the cultic side of priesthood, which still is mainly the Eucharist, is what sort of besots me the older I get. The word "Eucharist" means saying "Thank you." I think that God can never be thanked enough for being God
>
> and for sending his Son Jesus to be both God and a human being. There is no end to the amount of celebration which this warrants.

If the Incarnation—the Word become flesh—was the central truth of the Christian faith for Peter, he also celebrated in countless poems and sermons the joy and splendour of the Resurrection. He was ever conscious, however, that the path from Incarnation to Resurrection led through the divine vulnerability that climaxed at the cross. If Peter was a kind and compassionate priest, a faithful and sympathetic friend, it was so because he had personally plumbed and felt the brunt of human alienation and despair. He was no stranger to depression, could swiftly oscillate in mood between high and low.

For Peter the supreme moment of divine eloquence occurred at Calvary—an hour when the divine Son uttered very little but was stretched out, nailed and lifted from the earth in a helplessness of love eloquent beyond discourse of any kind. His 1986 poem *Crux* speaks so typically of Peter before that divine humility that I cannot forbear reading it now.

> Seeing you go
> Where the dead are bound, and having no resource
> To twist those timbers out of their lethal course,
> I want at least to know
>
> What I can say
> Now that the boasts have blown away and even
> The cursing has grown faint, while the pall of heaven
> Abolishes the day.
>
> I was never wise
> In word or silence, never understood
> The killer in my members, thought of good
> At what one might devise
>
> From scraps of evil.
> How can I learn a way for me or mine
> To stand beside you? Vinegar, not wine,
> Is all we give you still.
>
> Among the dice

> And the dirt, with more of shame than love to show,
> All that will come to heart is 'Do not go
> Alone to Paradise.'[42]

As he lay dying in Caritas Christi hospice last week, I asked him whether he remembered that poem.

"Indeed I do," he said. He was living—or rather, dying—it now.

As long as I've known him Peter has always lived in close consciousness of mortality. In the college library where we did our early studies in philosophy there weren't many books that were not in Latin. But Peter found his way to a treatise of Karl Rahner on death, and it left a mark upon his imagination and his writing that never went away. Nor was this preoccupation with mortality merely theoretical. I know there are many of you here present who have experienced Peter's priestly accompaniment through tragedy and loss in a deeply human way. Whether that was in the context of explicit Christian faith or no faith at all, Peter knew what to do and say. Of his own mortality, he said, again on that *Encounter* program:

> I believe it is a condition ... let's call it a room, which is what John Donne called it, which precedes and leads into a capacious and entirely blessed and secure immortality, one of whose names is heaven. And I believe in that very, very strongly. And I probably believe that more strongly than almost anything else.

To speak personally, it has always been a great sustenance for

---

[42] Published in *Marching on Paradise* (1986), and reprinted in Les Murray (ed.), *Australian Religious Poetry*; revised edition (Melbourne: Collins Dove: 1991), 140.

my own faith that Peter, who read everything, heard everything that could be thrown against the faith—in the name of so much suffering, so much evil—and who was constantly in conversation with friends and colleagues who did not share his faith, could hold to the end that "assurance of things hoped for, the conviction of things not seen" (Heb 11:1). Peter's faith was simple in the best sense, his piety unostentatious but profound. When you visited him in his room in the Dome of Newman College, there was his breviary open, his vow crucifix close at hand.

Many have remarked on the equanimity with which Peter accepted his terminal illness and the medical procedures it increasingly required. The poem *Rehearsal* is, I believe, his *Nunc Dimittis*. He addressed it publicly on several occasions in recent months, including what was to be in fact his last class of all, given to our Jesuit students at Jesuit Theological College early in May. Several times, in the course, of that event, granted his physical condition, I tried to bring the session to close but, try my best, he kept on explaining, drawing out responses—the teacher to the end.

The poem is too long to read here in full. Basically, it's a reverie while preparing (Peter the cook in action to the last!) the ingredients of a meal. He runs through all those places in a life of travel to which he must now say "Farewell." Here is the final stanza:

> But here's the mint still on my hands. A wreath,
> so Pliny thought, was "good for students,
> to exhilarate their minds." Late in the course,
> I'll settle for a sprig or two -
> the savour gracious, the leaves brimmingly green -
> as if never to say die.[43]

---
[43] *Rehearsal* from Peter Steele, *The Gossip and the Wine* (St Kilda, Victoria: John Leonard Press, 2010) 62.

Farewell, but once again the hint of resurrection.

The wreath motif must have appealed to Peter. It features also in a line from a poem he wrote to commemorate our mutual golden anniversary in the Society: "Yesterday's vow goes on wreathing its way through the heart."

Peter's vowed life as scholar, teacher, poet, priest, wit and friend has wreathed its way through our hearts—hearts that so keenly feel his loss. His immense legacy, in memory and print, will ensure that his eloquence about God remains.

Epilogue

Such then are the cast of twenty characters with whom I shared the divine comedy (in Dante's sense) of my life. More men and women, some of them high-octane personalities and others less so, could be cited. But these twenty, in various ways and with various intensity, shaped and nourished what I have become.

If I were to reflect on my enormous debt to my parents, I would find it hard to stop in spelling out all that they gave me. Let me mention only two lasting gifts. Father shared his commitment to institutions that enriched his life and through which he enriched others. He prepared the ground for my experiencing as lasting blessings many institutions: for instance, membership in the Catholic Church (from 1931), life in the Society of Jesus (from 1950), and teaching at the Gregorian University (1973–2006). Among innumerable ways Mother blessed me was her encouragement to study the classics and learn the languages in which they were written. Being able to read easily the New Testament in its original Greek has constantly offered spiritual nourishment.

The four popes who led the way in *Portraits* proved presences that illuminated my world. On Easter Sunday, year by passing year, I watched Paul VI, John Paul II, and Benedict XVI proclaiming *urbi et orbi* (to the city and the world) the heart of the Christian good news: the glorious resurrection of Jesus from the dead. His cruelly short pontificate prevented John Paul I from sharing himself with us even on one Easter Sunday. We can only imagine how this great communicator would have expressed the resurrection message.

With millions of other Catholics and Christians, I remain lastingly grateful to Paul VI for bringing to a happy conclusion the Second Vatican Council and doing his best to implement its teaching and reforms. I never regret dedicating much time with Dan Kendall and Jeff LaBelle in revisiting the teaching of John Paul II and producing a reader that can convey to others his rich legacy.[44] I drew valuable insights from the early writings of Cardinal Joseph Ratzinger. Later on, the investigation he led into the work of Jacques Dupuis proved, at least for me, a blessing in disguise. It forced me into thinking long and hard about major questions that enter interfaith dialogue. I continue to marvel at Pope Benedict's wisdom and courage in stepping down from the papacy.

Mother Teresa of Calcutta spoke up for the poorest of the poor; serving them truly means doing something beautiful for Christ. She prepared the way for the message I drew from Pope Francis: the poor must be heard when they speak their mind.

Thirteen other men and women feature in this book. They pulled their weight in providing direction for my life and keeping me going. They all gave me the feeling that they understood me and cared what happened to me. No one can ask for more than that from friends and relatives.

---

[44] *Pope John Paul II: A Reader* (Mahwah, NJ: Paulist Press, 2007).

Index of names

Adorno, Theodor 71
Aland, Kurt 219
Alfaro, Juan 62
Ali Agca, Mehemet 44, 51, 52
Amato, Cardinal Angelo 200
Andreotti, Giulio 66
Andropov, Yuri 140
Aquinas, St Thomas 72, 194
Aristotle 71
Armstrong, Neil 234
Arranz, Miguel 38
Arrupe, Pedro 16, 212–14
Athenagoras, Ecumenical Patriarch 19
Augustine of Canterbury, St 45
Augustine of Hippo, St 8, 71, 72

Baden-Powell, Baron Robert 92
Barry, Sir Redmond 101–2
Bartholomew, Ecumenical Patriarch 43
Batt, John 126
Bauckham, Richard 82
Belloc, Hilaire 161
Benedict XVI, Pope *passim*
Benelli, Cardinal Giovanni 154
Berchmans, St John 216
Bergman, Ingrid 133
Bergoglio, Cardinal Jorge *See* Francis, Pope
Berlin, Irving 144–45
Bernanos, Georges 32
Bertone, Cardinal Tarcisio 26, 73, 200

Bertrams, Wilhelm 16
Bogart, Humphrey 133
Boleyn, Anne 165
Bolt, Robert 234
Bonhoeffer, Dietrich 151
Borsellino, Paolo 140
Boylen, John Rolland ("Caesar") 133
Brooke, Rupert 165
Brookes, Sir Norman 95–7
Brother Andrew *See* Travers-Ball, Ian
Brown, Ralph 112
Brown, Raymond 63, 82
Bruce, (Viscount) Stanley 95–6
Burger, Henry 132–3
Burke, Edmund 91
Burns, Robert 112
Burns, Tom 29
Burridge, Richard 82
Burrows, William 195–6
Bush, President George W. 188
Byrne, Anne 238
Byrne, Brendan 9, 82, 204, 206–10, 235–43

Calder, Rosemary ("Posey") *See* O'Collins, Rosemary ("Posey")
Camara, Archbishop Helder 112, 153–4
Cappello, Anthony 9
Cappello, Felice 30, 36

247

Carey, Eileen 44, 142–3
Carey, Archbishop George 44–5, 142–3, 220
Carey, Rachel 220
Carroll, Archbishop John 187 n. 32
Casaroli, Cardinal Agostino 53, 154–5
Cassidy, Cardinal Edward 45
Catherine of Siena, St 72
Chadwick, Owen 182 n. 31
Chapman, Geoffrey 159–62
Chapman, Suzanne 160–2
Chenu, Marie-Dominique 203–4, 208
Chesterton, G. K. 161
Christina of Sweden, Queen 39, 57
Clifford, Bill 95
Coffey, Margaret 239
Congar, Yves 60, 208
Connelly, Sir Raymond 95–6
Constantine I, Emperor 82
Cornwell, John 37–8
Crock, Gerard 137
Crock, Harry 137

Dalai Lama, The 46, 191
Dalin, David 182 n. 31
Dallas Brooks, Sir Reginald 92
Damien of Molokai, Father *See* De Veuster, St Joseph
Dante Alighieri 233, 245
Davis, Stephen T. 142 n. 27
Del Gallo di Roccagiovine, Luigi 184
Demase, Isaac 9
Descartes, René 71

De Veuster, St Joseph 113
Dezza, Cardinal Paolo 22, 212
Divall, Richard 163–73
Donizetti, Gaetano 164
Donne, John 8, 241
Doria, Andrea 179
Doria Pamphilj, Prince Filippo Andrea 180–1
Doria Pamphilj, Princess Gesine 180
Doria Pogson Pamphilj, Prince Frank 141, 175–83, 226
Doria Pogson Pamphilj, Princess Gesine 9, 141–2, 175–7
Doria Pogson Pamphilj, Prince Jonathan 177
Doria Pogson Pamphilj, Princess Orietta 63, 175–84, 226–7
Dulles, Alan 188
Dulles, Cardinal Avery 62, 153, 185–89, 195
Dulles, John Foster 186
Dunn, James D. G. 82, 176
Dupuis, Jacques 65–7, 186, 191–202, 214–15, 246
Dyer, Reginald 94
Dynon, Abigail *See* Glynn, Abigail McMahon

Eco, Umberto 218
Eisenhower, President Dwight 186
Elizabeth II, Queen 164, 183
Elliott, Sister Fabian Wilhelmina 166
Etchegaray, Cardinal Roger 65

Falcone, Giovanni 140

Index of Names

Fangio, Juan 120
Farrugia, Mario 16 n. 1, 152 n. 30
Felici, Cardinal Pericle 41, 42
Festing, Grand Master Matthew 167
Festing, Michael Christian 167
Filippini, Josie 91
Fischer, Tim 126–7
Fitzgerald, Archbishop Michael 73
Fitzgerald, Paul 9
Fitzmyer, Joseph 63, 82
Flick, Maurizio 30
Follay, Bernard 75
Francis of Assisi, St 46
Francis, Pope 49, 69, 79, 144, 206, 208, 246
Fraser, Malcolm 130
Freeman, Cardinal James 33
Frings, Cardinal Josef 60

Gabriele, Paolo 79
Gagarin, Yuri 120
Gepp, Sir Herbert 99
Gielgud, John 55, 180
Gill, Kieran 9
Glynn, Abigail McMahon 101, 102
Glynn, Dympna 104
Glynn, Patrick McMahon 101–4, 108–9
Gnilka, Joachim 63
Gobbi, Tito 167
Gobbo, Sir James 165–6
Gobbo, Lady Shirley 165
Gorbachev, Mikhail 48
Gorbachev, Raissa 48

Grace of Monaco, Princess 153–4
Graham, Billy 43
Grattan, Hartley 90
Gray, Janette ("Jan") 9, 203–10
Gray, Roger 205–6
Gregory the Great, Pope (St) 44, 71, 220
Gregory, Lady Augusta 7
Griffiths, John 167–8
Grimwade, Major-General Harold 95
Gromyko, Andrei 38

Hammerstein, Oscar 133
Hammond, Dame Joan 164, 166–7, 171
Hanneken, Herman Henry 91–2
Hanrahan, Brian 59, 156
Harrington, Daniel 82
Harriott, John 24
Hart, Fritz 167
Hassan II, King 46
Hays, Richard 82
Heaney, Seamus 235
Henreid, Paul 133
Hildegard of Bingen, St 72
Hirschmann, Johannes 15–16
Hitchcock, Alfred 99
Hitler, Adolf 104
Hocking, Joseph 98–9
Hopkins, Gerard Manley 237
Hopman, Harry 96
Horsley, Charles 167
Howells, Ian 133
Hünermann, Peter 76–7
Hurley, Archbishop Denis 159

Ignatius Loyola, St 16, 24, 110,

249

151, 196, 220
Innocent X, Pope 179
Isouard, Nicolò 167–8

John XXIII, Pope (St) 15, 22, 24, 25 n. 1, 39, 76–7, 159, 182,
John of Austria, Don 74
John of Avila, St 72
John Paul I, Pope 29–39, 41–2, 57, 212–13, 245
John Paul II, Pope (St) *passim*
Johnson, Luke Timothy 82
Johnson, Samuel 233
Julian of Norwich, 162
Julius Caesar, 42
Jung, Carl Gustav 234

Kappler, Herbert 180
Kasper, Cardinal Walter 26
Keating, Thomas 229
Keener, Craig 82
Kelly, Frederick Septimus 165, 167
Kelly, Ned 101–2
Kendall, Daniel 68, 104 n. 22, 142 n. 27, 246
Kennedy, President John 227
Kennedy, Ethel 227
Kennedy, Robert 227
King, Geoffrey 209
Kirby, Edward ("Ed") 92
Knox, Cardinal James 19, 151
Knox, Ronald 161
Kolvenbach, Peter-Hans 67, 197, 200, 211–16
König, Cardinal Franz 66, 195,
197–9, 201
Küng, Hans 119
Kwitny, Jonathan 37 n. 7

LaBelle, Jeffrey 68, 246
Langer, Bernard 100
Latourelle, René 59–60, 62, 192
Lash, Nicholas 204
Lee, Dorothy 82
Lefebvre, Archbishop Marcel 75, 76
Leo the Great, Pope St 220
Léon-Dufour, Xavier 63
Lewis, Deirdre 135–6
Lindbeck, George 176
Lindbergh, Charles 187
Little, Archbishop Sir Frank 221
Lohse, Eduard 63, 176, 226
Luciani, Cardinal Albino *See* John Paul I, Pope
Luther, Martin 45, 107
Luz, Ulrich 82
Lynch, Phillip 139

Macdougall, A. K. 95 n. 8, 110 n. 23
Maciel Degollado, Marcial 53
Mackerras, Sir Charles 167
Magee, Bishop John 21, 52
Malatrasi, Rina 118
Manion, Margaret 238
Manuel II Palaeologus, Emperor 73
Marcus, Joel 82
Marini, Archbishop Piero 56
Marshall, John 17–18
Marshall-Hall, G. W. 167

Index of Names

Martini, Cardinal Carlo Maria 24, 26, 41, 53, 62–3, 217–22
Martinez Somalo, Cardinal 64
Mary Magdalene, St 104
Mary, Queen of Scots 106, 164
McCarthy, Eugene ("Gene") 223–9
McCarthy, John 224
McCarthy, Joseph 224
McCarthy, Maureen 223–9
McCarthy, Paul 224
McCarthy, Robert ("Butter") 132–3
McCaughey, Patrick 233
McMahon, Paul 9
McTiernan, Sir Edward 90–1
Meier, John 82
Melba, Dame Nellie 96
Melville, Ken 137
Metz, Johann Baptist 62
Mills, Richard 164, 173
Minh Tran 123
Moloney, Francis 82
Moltmann, Jürgen 119, 151–2
Monash, Sir John 110 n. 23
Muggeridge, Malcolm 150 n. 29, 153
Muhammad 73, 74
Murdoch, Rupert 95 n. 19
Murphy, Jeremiah 136, 138
Murphy, Roland 63
Murphy-O'Connor, Jerome 112
Murray, Les 240 n. 42
Mussolini, Benito 181
Myers, Allan 165
Myers, Maria 165

Nathan, Isaac 167
Neumann, Balthasar 107
Neuner, Josef 193
Neusner, Jacob 81
Newman, Blessed John Henry 17, 151
Nguyen, Joseph 214
Nguyen Van Thuan, Cardinal 71
Niall, Brenda 103 n. 20
Nicolás, Adolfo 213
Nietzsche, Friedrich Wilhelm 71
Nightingale, Florence 109
Nikodim, Metropolitan 38
Nineham, Dennis 17
Nineham, Ruth 17

O'Collins, Alice 87
O'Collins, Dympna 89, 94, 106, 129
O'Collins, Ellen 87, 88 n. 15
O'Collins, Glynn 94, 95, 129, 131–6
O'Collins, James ("Jamie") 141–2
O'Collins, Bishop James Patrick 87, 104–6, 109, 133–5, 139
O'Collins, James Patrick ("Jim") 94, 129, 131–45
O'Collins, Joan 101–13, 116, 120, 129, 132, 138, 245
O'Collins, Maev 9, 89, 94, 110, 135–6
O'Collins, Margaret ("Mollie") 87

O'Collins, Michael Fitzgerald ("Gerald") 87, 109
O'Collins, Moira *See* Peters, Moira
O'Collins, Patrick ("Pat") 87
O'Collins, Patrick Francis ("Frank") 87
O'Collins, Rosemary ("Posey") 9, 139–43, 145
O'Collins, Victoria ("Tori") 141–2
O'Collins, William ("Will") 87, 105
O'Flaherty, Hugh 180
O'Kelly, Bishop Greg 208

Paisley, Ian 102–3
Park, Jin-hyuk 9
Parker, Elizabeth 9
Patterson, Gerald 96–7
Paul VI, Pope (St) 15–27, 30, 38–9, 45, 57, 59, 72, 77, 182, 196, 212, 220, 245–6
Pavarotti, Luciano 167
Peck, Gregory 180
Pell, Cardinal George 221
Perkins, Pheme 82
Peters, Bronwen 9, 119
Peters, James Sturrock 89, 116–23, 125, 129, 135
Peters, James W. S. 9, 119
Peters, Joanna 119
Peters, Justin 9, 119
Peters, Marion 9, 118, 125
Peters, Mark 9, 119–21, 123–4,
Peters, Moira 89, 94, 106, 115–29, 135
Peters, Stephen 119
Peters, Stewart 9, 118, 127
Pittau, Archbishop Joseph 211–12
Pius V, Pope (St) 25 n. 1, 77

Pius XI, Pope 16
Pius XII, Pope 16, 181–2
Plato 71
Plummer, Christopher 180
Poe, Edgar Allan 103
Pongratz-Lippitt, Christa 198, 201
Porter, Peter 233
Potter, Lady Primrose 165–6

Quinn, Anthony 125–6

Rahner, Karl 62, 156, 241
Rainier of Monaco, Prince 153–4
Rains, Claude 133
Raleigh, Sir Walter 93
Ramsey, Archbishop Michael 16–17, 23, 45, 182
Ratzinger, Joseph *See* Benedict XVI, Pope
Ratzinger, Maria 61
Ricciarelli, Katia 167
Richard of Chichester, St 143, 145
Richardson, Henry Handel 167
Riordan, Ned 236
Roosevelt, Eleanor 92
Rosmini-Serbati, Blessed Antonio 30
Ross, Alexander 9, 171
Runcie, Archbishop Robert 63, 182

Schnackenburg, Rudolf 63
Schneiders, Sandra 82
Schürmann, Heinz 63
Schutz, Roger 56–7
Scofield, Paul 111

Index of Names

Segal, Eric 187
Semmelroth, Otto 15–16
Shakespeare, William 42, 103
Shaw, Jack 138
Sheed, Frank 161
Shepherd, Lemuel C. 92
Siddons, Sarah 111
Smith, David 48
Smythe, Harry 23
Stalin, Joseph 48
Stanley, Francis O. 137 n. 26
Stanley, Freelan E. 137 n26
Steele, Peter 9, 231–43
Swift, Jonathan 232
Synge, J. M. 7

Tagore, Rabindrinath 94, 175
Tennyson, Lord Alfred 115
Tensing, Sherpa 191
Teresa of Avila, St 72, 224
Teresa of Calcutta, Mother (St) 42, 149–57, 246
Thérèse of Lisieux, St 72
Thompson, John 102 n. 12
Toaff, Elio 57–8
Tobagi, Stella 219
Tobagi, Walter 218–19
Toppo, Cardinal Telesphore Placidus 50
Torrell, Jean-Pierre 62
Travers-Ball, Ian 151
Turkson, Cardinal Peter Kodwo Appiah 50
Turnbull, Malcolm 221
Tutu, Archbishop Desmond 161

Vanhoye, Cardinal Albert 63, 64
Vaughan, Gerard 233

Velázquez 179
Verdi, Giuseppe 164
Villot, Cardinal Jean-Marie 19, 38–9
Virgil 71
Von Richthofen, Baron Manfred 110–11
Vorgrimler, Herbert 60

Wako, Cardinal Gabriel Zubeir 49
Wallace-Crabbe, Christopher 234
Ward, Maisie 161
Ware, Bishop Kallistos 52
Waugh, Evelyn 161
Wayne, John 52
Wellington, Duke of 32
Wesley, Charles 167
Wesley, John 151
Wicks, Jared 60
Wilkins, John 9, 25, 77 n. 13, 79, 196–202
Willcock, Christopher 8
Willebrands, Cardinal Jan 23
Williamson, Richard 75, 76 n. 12
Wojtyla, Cardinal Karol *See* John Paul II, Pope (St)
Woodward, Kenneth 227
Wordsworth, William 115
Wright, Sir Roy Douglas ("Pansy") 137
Wright, N. T. 82

Yallop, David 36–8
Yeats, W. B. 7, 108

Zeffirelli, Franco 20

www.ingramcontent.com/pod-product-compliance
Lightning Source LLC
Chambersburg PA
CBHW052058300426
44117CB00013B/2191